ACADEMIC
CONNECTIONS 2

ACADEMIC CONNECTIONS 2

DAVID HILL

PEARSON
Longman

Academic Connections 2

Copyright © 2010 by Pearson Education, Inc.
All rights reserved.

No part of this publication may be reproduced, stored in a retrieval system, or transmitted in any form, or by any means, electronic, mechanical, photocopying, recording, or otherwise, without the prior permission of the publisher.

Pearson Education, 10 Bank Street, White Plains, NY 10606

Staff credits: The people who made up the *Academic Connections 2* team, representing editorial, production, design, and manufacturing, are Pietro Alongi, Andrew Blasky, Aerin Csigay, Christine Edmonds, Ann France, Gosia Jaros-White, Caroline Kasterine, Sherry Preiss, Karen Quinn, Robert Ruvo, Debbie Sistino, and Paula Van Ells.

ETS staff credits: The ETS people who made up the *Academic Connections* team, representing research, test design and scoring, item development, statistical analysis, and literature reviews, are Matthew Chametzky, Terry Cryan, Phil Everson, Elizabeth Jenner, Kate Kazin, Dawn Leusner, Brad Moulder, Jan Plante, Jonathon Schmidt, and Jody Stern.

Project editors: John Beaumont, Nan Clarke
Cover art: Art on File/Corbis
Text composition: Kirchoff/Wohlberg, Inc.
Text font: 11/13 Times Roman
Reviewers: See page xxiv

Library of Congress Cataloging-in-Publication Data

Academic connections. -- 1st ed.
    p. cm.
  ISBN 0-13-233843-2 (Level 1) -- ISBN 0-13-233844-0 (Level 2) -- ISBN 0-13-233845-9
(Level 3) -- ISBN 0-13-233841-6 (Level 4) 1. English language--Rhetoric--Problems, exercises, etc. 2. Report writing--Problems, exercises, etc. 3. Listening--Problems, exercises, etc. 4. Reading comprehension--Problems, exercises, etc. 5. College readers. I. Cassriel, Betsy. II. Martisen, Marit ter Mate III. Hill, David. IV. Williams, Julia
  PE1408.A223 2010
  428.0071'1--dc22

                                       2009017781

ISBN-10: 0-13-233844-0
ISBN-13: 978-0-13-233844-8

Printed in the United States of America
2 3 4 5 6 7 8 9 10—V011—14 13 12 11 10

CONTENTS

WELCOME TO **ACADEMIC CONNECTIONS**

Academic Connections is a four-level, integrated skills course designed for students **preparing for academic study** as well as for **standardized tests**. A systematic, building-block approach helps students develop and sharpen their language skills as well as their academic and test-taking abilities.

The ACADEMIC CONNECTIONS Series Is

INTEGRATED

- *Academic Connections* **integrates** all four language skills—reading, listening, writing, and speaking.
- *Academic Connections* teaches students **how to integrate skills** and **content** in real-world academic contexts.
- **Integration of various media** empowers students and instills confidence.

ACADEMIC

- Academic skills and content prepare students for **success in the classroom** and on **standardized tests**.
- Explicit, **step-by-step skill development** leads to student mastery. With careful instruction and engaging practice tasks, students learn how to **organize information**, **make connections**, and **think critically**.
- Key **academic skills** are introduced, reinforced, and expanded in all four levels to facilitate acquisition.

AUTHENTIC

- **High-interest** and **intellectually stimulating authentic material** familiarizes students with content they will encounter in academic classes. Readings and lectures are excerpted or adapted from textbooks, academic journals, and other academic sources.

- Course content covers five **academic content areas**: Social Science, Life Science, Physical Science, Business and Marketing, and Arts and Literature.

- **Authentic tasks**, including listening to lectures, note-taking, participating in debates, preparing oral and written reports, and writing essays, prepare students for the demands of the content class.

ASSESSMENT-BASED

Academic Connections provides a **variety of assessments** that result in more effective student practice opportunities based upon individual needs:

- A *placement* test situates students in the appropriate level.
- *Pre-course* and *post-course* tests allow teachers to target instruction and measure achievement.
- *Multi-unit* tests track individual and class progress.
- *Formative assessments* monitor student skill mastery, allowing teachers to assign individualized exercises focused on the specific learning needs of the class.

RESEARCH-BASED

- *Academic Connections* was developed in cooperation with the **Educational Testing Service (ETS)**, creators of the TOEFL® test. The blend of curriculum and assessment is based on research that shows when English language learners are provided with authentic tasks, individualized and target practice opportunities, and timely feedback, they are better able to develop and integrate their reading, writing, speaking, and listening skills.

PERSONALIZED

MyAcademicConnectionsLab, an easy-to-use **online** learning and assessment program, is an integral part of the *Academic Connections* series.

MyAcademicConnectionsLab offers:

- **Unlimited access** to reading and listening selections with online glossary support.
- **Original activities** that support the *Academic Connections* program. These include activities that build academic skills and vocabulary.
- **Focused test preparation** to help students succeed academically and on international exams. Regular **formative** and **summative assessments**, developed by ETS experts, provide evidence of student learning and progress.
- **Individualized instruction**, **instant feedback**, and **personalized study** plans help students improve results.
- **Time-saving tools** include a **flexible gradebook** and **authoring features** that give teachers **control of content** and help them **track student progress**.

THE **ACADEMIC CONNECTIONS** UNIT

UNIT OPENER

Each unit in the *Academic Connections* series begins with a captivating opener that outlines the unit's content, academic skills, and requirements. The outline mirrors an authentic academic syllabus and conveys the unit's academic purpose.

The content in *Academic Connections* is organized around five academic disciplines: Social Sciences, Life Sciences, Physical Sciences, Business and Marketing, and Arts and Literature.

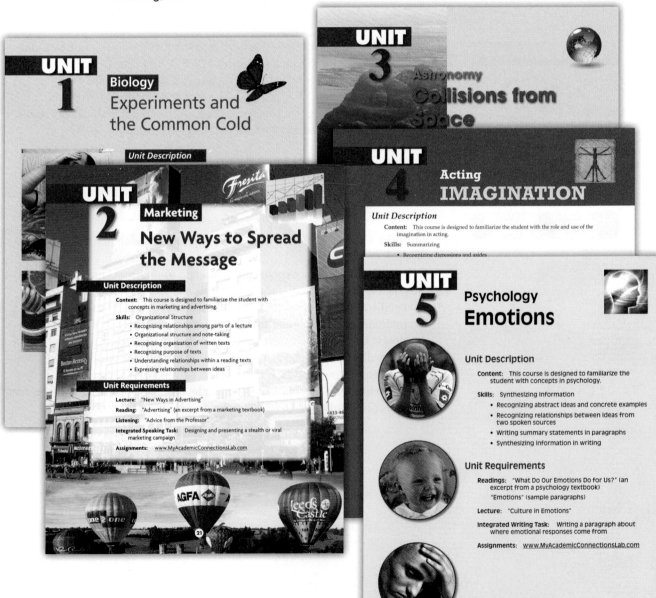

UNIT 1
Biology
Experiments and the Common Cold

Unit Description

UNIT 3
Astronomy
Collisions from Space

UNIT 4
Acting
IMAGINATION

Unit Description
Content: This course is designed to familiarize the student with the role and use of the imagination in acting.
Skills: Summarizing
- Recognizing digressions and asides

UNIT 2
Marketing
New Ways to Spread the Message

Unit Description

Content: This course is designed to familiarize the student with concepts in marketing and advertising.
Skills: Organizational Structure
- Recognizing relationships among parts of a lecture
- Organizational structure and note-taking
- Recognizing organization of written texts
- Recognizing purpose of texts
- Understanding relationships within a reading texts
- Expressing relationships between ideas

Unit Requirements

Lecture: "New Ways in Advertising"
Reading: "Advertising" (an excerpt from a marketing textbook)
Listening: "Advice from the Professor"
Integrated Speaking Task: Designing and presenting a stealth or viral marketing campaign
Assignments: www.MyAcademicConnectionsLab.com

UNIT 5
Psychology
Emotions

Unit Description

Content: This course is designed to familiarize the student with concepts in psychology.

Skills: Synthesizing Information
- Recognizing abstract ideas and concrete examples
- Recognizing relationships between ideas from two spoken sources
- Writing summary statements in paragraphs
- Synthesizing information in writing

Unit Requirements

Readings: "What Do Our Emotions Do for Us?" (an excerpt from a psychology textbook)
"Emotions" (sample paragraphs)

Lecture: "Culture in Emotions"

Integrated Writing Task: Writing a paragraph about where emotional responses come from

Assignments: www.MyAcademicConnectionsLab.com

1

Preview

This section introduces students to the theme of the unit.

Previewing the Academic Content gives an overview of the topic, engages students in it, and exposes them to key words they will need in order to proceed.

This unit will help you to see and follow the organizational structure of lectures, essays, and other academic texts.

Previewing the Academic Skills Focus

Organizational Structure

Organizational structure is the pattern of ideas across the text or lecture. Many lectures, essays, and academic textbook sections in English follow the same basic structure:

- The **introduction** gives the main idea of the text. It opens the topic with important general information (**the general statement**). The introduction also gives the main idea(s) of the text (**the scope**). The general statement and scope can be one or more sentences in length.
- The **body** gives more specific information about the main idea. It gives explanations, examples, reasons, effects, etc.
- The **conclusion** returns to the main idea presented in the introduction and closes the topic.

The introduction and the conclusion are usually short. The body is the longer, main part of the text.

Recognizing the organizational structure can help you to follow the main ideas throughout a lecture or reading. When you give talks or write essays, organizing your ideas into a structure can help people understand you clearly.

1. Read the introduction to a chapter in a marketing textbook. Underline the general statement once and the scope twice.

> IN THIS CHAPTER, we'll look at how to get advertisements into the right place at the right time for the right people to see them. First, we'll look at things like the type of medium—which kind of magazine or TV show is the best place to advertise a particular product. After that, we'll move on to the timing of ad campaigns. This includes the time of day in the case of radio, TV, and the Internet, and also the time of the week and the season of the year. We'll finish by looking at new ways that people get their message to their customers. We'll see that clever companies do more than use just traditional advertising.

2. Work with a partner. Discuss the questions.
1. What main ideas will come up later in the unit?
2. Which ideas might the conclusion mention?

1

Preview

For online assignments, go to

Previewing the Academic Content

Water is extremely important for our lives—not just for drinking, but also for growing our food. Too much of it, and we have floods; too little, and we have drought. There is a natural cycle—the hydrologic cycle—that generally gives us the right amount of water. But if we disturb the cycle, disasters happen.

In this unit, we will look at some of these disasters and find out how they happened. From this, we will know how to avoid the same problems in the future.

1. Study the key words and the pictures. Then write the key words under the correct pictures.

a. _____   c. _____

b. _____

d. _____   e. _____

Key Words

drought *n* a time when there is very little rain and growing food becomes difficult

dry up *v* to lose water or moisture over a period of time

erosion *n* damage caused by rain and wind on a natural surface; over time, erosion can cause areas of land to disappear or change shape; **erode** *v*

flood *n* water covering an area that is usually dry, such as houses or farm land

tropical cyclone *n* a very powerful storm, with very strong winds and heavy rain. Tropical storms that start in the Atlantic Ocean are called **hurricanes** and ones that start in the western Pacific, near East Asia, are called **typhoons**.

2. Work with a partner. Read an excerpt from a newspaper report. Discuss what consequences of the event might happen for:
- people who stay behind in their homes
- business owners
- farmers

STORM PREPARATIONS CONTINUE

People in Tai Zhou, China, are securing their homes and preparing to leave as the storm predicted for Friday night nears. Up to 15 inches (38 cm) of rain is expected, with winds of over 93 miles (150 km) per hour. It is expected to be several days before people can return to their homes.

Previewing the Academic Skills Focus gives an overview of the academic skill for the unit. The material activates students' awareness of the skill and then prompts them to use it on a global level.

2 and 3

Building Academic Reading and Listening Skills

Sections 2 and 3 focus on academic reading and listening skills. First, students read a text or listen to a lecture on a topic related to the unit's academic discipline. They acquire reading and listening skills through careful instruction and engaging practice tasks.

Every unit includes both reading and listening.

Before You Read/Listen introduces students to the topic of the selection with pre-reading or pre-listening activities. The activities may include discussions that activate students' prior knowledge of the topic; they may also include vocabulary or brief academic skill practice.

MyAcademicConnectionsLab icons remind students to complete their online assignments.

---

2 Building Academic Reading Skills

In this section, you will practice differentiating between abstract ideas and concrete examples. For online assignments, go to

Key Words

blood vessels *n* the tubes that blood flows through, all around the body

brain *n* the part of a person inside the head that controls the body and thinks

breathing *n* the action of letting air in and out of the body; **breathe** *v*

lungs *n* the two large parts of the body that take in and let out air and allow air to enter the blood

physically *adv* connected with a person's body, not their mind; **physical** *adj*

respond *v* take action as a result of something that happens (e.g., you might respond to touching something hot by dropping it); **response** *n*

Before You Read

1. *Think about a stressful event that you have experienced, such as an exam or being late for an appointment. Then tell a partner.*

   1. What was the event?

   2. How did you feel physically and emotionally?

   3. How did you want to respond at that moment?

2. *Work with a partner. First, read the list of physical responses that happen when a person experiences strong emotions such as fear. Then look at Figure 5.1. Label the places in the body with the physical responses from the list.*

Physical Responses

- Sweating increases
- Heart beats faster and stronger
- Brain becomes more alert
- Lungs get ready to take in more air
- Breathing becomes faster
- Skin becomes whiter because the blood vessels become narrower
- Sight becomes more sensitive
- Hearing becomes more sensitive

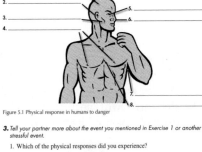

1. _____
2. _____
3. _____
4. _____
5. _____
6. _____
7. _____
8. _____

Figure 5.1 Physical response in humans to danger

3. *Tell your partner more about the event you mentioned in Exercise 1 or another stressful event.*

   1. Which of the physical responses did you experience?

   2. What physical responses do you generally experience in stressful situations?

   3. What can you do to control these responses?

   4. Why do you think humans have emotions? Explain.

 Unit 5 ■ Emotions   **77**

---

3. *Work with a partner. Discuss the possible purposes for each item. Think of more than one purpose for each.*

   1. an advertisement for a play

   2. a student's notes, taken during a literature lecture

   3. a student essay

2 Building Academic Listening Skills

In this section, you will practice recognizing a speaker's attitude. For online assignments, go to

Key Words

colony *n*
generation *n*
influence *n*
missionary *n*
religion *n*
theme *n*

Before You Listen

1. *Read the encyclopedia entry about Chinua Achebe.*

Chinua Achebe (pronounced: /ˈtʃɪnwɑː əˈtʃɛbeɪ/) is a novelist and poet from Nigeria. His first novel, *Things Fall Apart*, is one of the most famous and widely read African novels. Achebe was born in 1930, when Nigeria was still a British colony. His early experiences have been a major influence on his work and provide many of the themes in his stories. Christian missionaries from Britain were very active in the part of Nigeria where he grew up. As a result, many people of his generation and older grew up with a mixture of the local religion and Christianity.

2. *Find the words in the biography of Chinua Achebe. Determine their meaning from the context. Write the words next to their definitions.*

   1. _____ all the people who were born at around the same time

   2. _____ a belief in one or more gods, and the behaviors that go with this belief (e.g., going to a special building on a certain day of the week)

   3. _____ a topic that we see several times in a piece of literature

   4. _____ a country or area that is controlled by another country

   5. _____ someone who goes to another country and tries to make people believe his or her religion

   6. _____ have an effect on something

114 Unit 7 ■ Literature

---

x   Welcome to *Academic Connections*

Global Reading

1. Skim the text quickly. Number the ideas in the order they appear. Then compare your answers with a partner's.

_____ There were ideas for their disappearance, but there was little evidence.

__1__ The dinosaurs' disappearance was mysterious and sudden.

_____ Could the same happen to us?

_____ A layer of iridium was discovered, which is evidence for the meteorite theory.

_____ The Chicxulub crater provided further evidence for the meteorite theory.

_____ No one knows how often these major catastrophes happen.

_____ A large meteorite can kill living things all around the world.

What Killed the Dinosaurs?

The Biggest Mystery in Earth's History
1 For many years, one of the biggest mysteries in science has been how the dinosaurs disappeared.

2 These amazing animals ruled Earth for 160 million years. They lived everywhere, on every continent. They were the largest and most powerful animals for a large part of the history of animal life on Earth. Compared with humans' two hundred thousand years or so, this is an amazing achievement. But, suddenly, about 65 million years ago, they all died. And it wasn't just the dinosaurs—interestingly, more than 50 percent of all animal species on Earth also disappeared. This is very surprising,

because there were very many different species of dinosaur, all suited to different climates and conditions. The normal causes of extinction, such as natural climate change, may explain why some species of dinosaur died out, but not all of them. As we will see, it seems likely that a major and sudden disaster caused their disappearance.

A Solution . . . Perhaps
3 So, what was this disaster? In the past, scientists thought of many possible explanations. These included disease, earthquakes, volcanoes, or even changes in the magnetic field of Earth. Unfortunately, for a long time, there was no strong evidence for any of them.

4 This changed, however, in 1980. Researchers, led by Nobel Prize winner Luis Alvarez, noticed something unusual. To help us explain what this

(continued on next page)

Global Listening

1. ⌂ Listen to the lecture. Who speaks about these ideas? Write **P** (the professor), **G** (the guest speaker), or **X** (not mentioned). Then compare your answers with a partner's.

_____ 1. Gene Blake's experience

_____ 2. a definition of the word *imagination*

_____ 3. why imagination is important

_____ 4. how to start preparing for a new role

_____ 5. example of a disabled character

_____ 6. celebration and partying

_____ 7. a character from a book

_____ 8. using personal experience

Recognizing Digressions and Asides

Sometimes lecturers go off their main point (**digressions**) or tell stories that are related to the point but not an important part of it (**asides**). They do this to make the talk interesting.

It is important to recognize when the lecturer is digressing or giving an aside, and when the lecturer is making a major point. Digressions and asides often sound like small stories rather than statements of fact.

Do not include digressions or asides in summaries.

2. Work with a partner. Which point from Exercise 1 is a digression or an aside?

3. Work with a partner. What is the lecture mainly about? Write two or three sentences in your notebook to summarize the lecture.

Focused Listening

1. ⌂ The following statements are false. Read them and then listen to the first part of the lecture. Change each statement to make it true. Then compare your answers with a partner's.

1. Gene Blake now teaches master classes at theaters around the world.

_____

2. Imagination is any process in which we talk about anything that we are not currently experiencing.

_____

3. Imagination can be based on personal experience only.

_____

In **Focused Reading/Listening**, students begin to explore the complexities of the selection. Comprehension, critical thinking, and/or inference activities in this section test students' detailed understanding of the text and lecture. This section might introduce another academic skill related to reading/listening and offer practice of the skill.

At the end of Sections 2 and 3, students are prompted to take an online test on **MyAcademicConnectionsLab**. These section tests (Checkpoints) monitor student progress and allow the teacher to assign individualized exercises focused on students' specific needs.

Focused Listening

1. 🎧 Listen to an excerpt from the lecture. As you listen to the description of a natural water cycle, check off (✓) the arrows on the diagram on page 136.

2. 🎧 Listen to another excerpt from the lecture. As you listen to the description of what happens when humans interfere in the water cycle, cross out the arrows that show the flow that decreases, and circle the arrows showing the flow that increases.

3. 🎧 Work with a partner. Look at the cause-effect diagram. Predict where the words and expressions from the box fit in the digram. Then listen to check and complete your answers.

~~cutting down trees~~	filtration stops; water runs directly to waterways	more sediment and pollution
~~erosion~~	floods	overuse of land

CAUSES → **CHAIN OF EFFECTS**

- cutting down trees
- _____

→ - _____

→ - erosion

→ - _____

4. 🎧 Work with the same partner. Look at the cause-effect diagram on page 138. Predict where the expressions from the box fit in the diagram. Then listen to check and complete your answers.

bottom of river rises	more erosion	~~more floods~~	more sediment
less filtering of water	more farming	more tree cutting	~~worse floods~~

(continued on next page)

Drawing Conclusions

In your academic studies, you will have to draw conclusions. **Drawing a conclusion** means looking at all the information you have about a topic and making a guess or forming an opinion about that information. Your conclusion is an inference based on the information you have.

By drawing conclusions, you can show that you understand ideas and form opinions based on these ideas.

To draw conclusions:

- Look at all the information you can find. Look for connections and patterns in this information. Try to think of consequences, ideas for future actions, or solutions to problems. These are your conclusions.
- Check again that your conclusions fit the facts. Remember that a conclusion is usually a guess or an opinion that is based on information given.

3. Work with a partner. Based on information in the reading, what conclusions can you draw? Think about future actions, consequences, and possible solutions to problems.

1. The governments of Kazakhstan and Uzbekistan should *take action quickly. They need to repair the damage to the Aral Sea. They need to find something to replace the cotton industry—something that needs less water. They also should* _____

2. The governments of other, wealthier, countries should _____

3. People living in the area should _____

4. Farmers and people responsible for irrigation projects should _____

Checkpoint 1 PEARSON LONGMAN myacademicconnectionslab 🛒

4

Building Academic Writing/ Speaking Skills

This section emphasizes development of productive skills for writing or speaking. It presents language and academic skills needed for the integrated task. Students also read or listen to another selection that expands on or otherwise complements the earlier selections.

Each unit concludes with an integrated writing or speaking task based on the authentic needs of the academic classroom. Units alternate between focusing on writing and speaking.

Before You Write/Speak introduces the language skill that students will need in the integrated task.

4

Building Academic Writing Skills

In this section, you will practice writing summary statements and synthesizing information. Then you will write about emotions and emotional expression using information from the readings and the lecture in this unit. For online assignments, go to myacademicconnectionslab

Before You Write

1. Read the paragraph. The main idea is stated twice. Underline each one. Identify the topic sentence.

> Some emotional responses appear to be biologically "built in" to every human. Some of the evidence for this comes from research by Irenäus Eibl-Eibesfeldt. In the early '70s, he devised a natural experiment to test this hypothesis. His study included babies who had been blind since birth. He watched their emotional expressions over the first few months of their life. It was clear that they smiled, frowned, and cried just like other children. Clearly they could not have learned these responses by watching their parents, because they could not see them. Thus, it is clear that these responses are biological, not learned from other people.
>
> Source: Adapted from Zimbardo, P., Johnson, R. L., Weber, A. L., & Gruber, C. W. (2007). Psychology, AP Edition. Upper Saddle River, NJ: Pearson Prentice Hall.

Writing Summary Statements in Paragraphs

Many paragraphs have a statement at the end, which summarizes the main idea. It is often a good idea to include a summary statement because it helps to make the main idea clear. However, not all paragraphs have a summary statement. For example, they are not as useful for introductory paragraphs of essays or in short paragraphs. Only write summary statements where you think they are useful.

2. Read the two paragraphs. Decide which one needs a summary statement most. Discuss your answer with a partner. Then write a summary statement for the paragraph you chose.

Sample Paragraph 1

> How many emotions are there? A long look at the dictionary turns up more than 500 emotional terms. Most experts, however, see a small number of basic emotions. Ekman lists six or seven, which you have already come across. Robert Plutchik's research suggests that there might be eight basic emotions. Plutchik's list is very similar to Ekman's. But what about emotions that are not on either list? One theory says that each emotion is a combination of the basic emotions. For example, disappointment is a mixture of sadness and surprise.

(continued on next page)

4

Building Academic Speaking Skills

In this section, you will practice expressing relationships between ideas. Then you will plan a marketing campaign, using either viral marketing or stealth marketing. You will use information from the reading and the lecture in this unit and from a radio talk you will hear to complete the task. For online assignments, go to myacademicconnectionslab

Before You Speak

You will hear a professor giving students some advice about their assignment. The assignment is to plan a stealth or viral marketing campaign.

🎧 Listen and take notes in the middle column. Then listen again and write the logical connectives you hear in the right-hand column. Compare your chart with a partner's.

	What Does the Professor Say about the Message?	Logical Connectives
Point 1		
Point 2		
Strategy 1 (Point 2)		
Strategy 2 (Point 2)		

Focused Speaking

You are going to give a short talk of one to two minutes to practice using signals and logical connectives.

Expressing Relationships between Ideas

Just like the professors you hear, you should use signals and logical connectives in your talks. This will make the organizational structure, and the relationships between ideas, clear.

1. Work with a partner. Choose one of the topics. Brainstorm ideas.
- three reasons to buy a product
- three things a business can do to make people want to buy a product
- three things a website can do to make people want to buy a product

---

2. *When you next hear on the news about an asteroid passing close to Earth, what will you think? Choose one of the opinions, or write your own. Share your opinion with the class.*
- "The news is making it sound more dangerous than it really is."
- "I wish the government would spend more money on NEO research."
- Your opinion: _____

Focused Writing

Writing Cohesive Texts

Cohesion is important in writing. Remember to use techniques for cohesion, including referencing and logical connectives in your writing.

1. *Read the text. Complete the sentences with the words from the box. Some words are not used, and some are used more than once.*

however	later	this
in addition	they	to conclude

Early one morning in June 1908, some of the few people near the forests of Tunguska, in north central Siberia, heard a strange noise. When they looked up, they saw a bright light, nearly as bright as the sun, moving quickly across the sky. A few minutes after (1) _____*this*_____, there was a bright flash and a very loud noise. (2) _____ was quickly followed by a shock wave that broke windows hundreds of miles away. For a few days after (3) _____ event, nights were so bright that people could read without lights. Fortunately, (4) _____ happened in a very remote area with very few people.

(5) _____, an expedition of scientists went to Tunguska to make maps. (6) _____ could easily see that a big disaster had happened, because for around 30 miles (50 kilometers), all the trees were flat on the ground. (7) _____ guessed that a meteorite had caused it. (8) _____, it was not until near the end of the twentieth century that this was confirmed. What most likely happened was that a large meteorite, about 200 feet (60 meters) across, got so hot that it exploded, about 5 miles (8 kilometers) above Earth.

Focused Writing/Speaking explains the skill that will be used in the integrated task. Students use the additional reading or listening selection in this section to practice the skill and prepare for the integrated task activity.

Focused Speaking

1. *Look at the steps for preparing spoken summaries in the box. How useful do you think each step is? Discuss your ideas with a partner.*

Preparing Spoken Summaries

Here is a suggested process for preparing spoken summaries:
- **Step 1:** Note the main ideas of the text(s) you are summarizing.
- **Step 2:** Make notes of your main ideas without looking at your source texts.
- **Step 3:** Check your notes against the source texts. Change them if necessary.
- **Step 4:** Practice your spoken summary with a partner.
- **Step 5:** Discuss how to improve your summary. Change your notes if necessary.
- **Step 6:** Practice again by yourself or with a partner.

Speaking from notes is better than writing every word, because preparation is quicker and you will sound more natural when speaking.

2a. *Prepare an oral summary to answer this question:* **How can actors use imagination to improve their performance?** *Follow the steps in the skills box above. Note that you have already completed part of Step 1 in the outline on page 65. Add notes if you like.*

2b. *Work with a partner. Listen to each other's summaries. While listening, complete the checklist.*

Does the summary include. . .	Yes
all major points?	
only important details?	
the speaker's own words?	

3. *Continue working with your partner. Give each other feedback. Use the checklist to help you answer the questions.*
- Whose summary was shorter?
- Were any important ideas missing?
- How can you improve your presentation?

4. *Using a similar process, prepare a summary of the movie synopsis you read.*

The **Integrated Writing/Speaking Task** challenges students to organize and synthesize information from the reading and listening selections in a meaningful way. Students follow clear steps that require them to use the vocabulary and academic skills they have learned in the unit. Completing the task is a productive achievement that gives students the tools and the confidence needed for academic success.

Integrated Writing Task

You have listened to a lecture about Nigerian life as it relates to Chinua Achebe and his writing, read an excerpt from *Marriage Is a Private Affair*, and heard a summary about it. You will now use your knowledge of the content, vocabulary, purpose, essay writing, and audience to write a four-paragraph essay in response to this question: **Clashes between the modern and the traditional have been an important theme both in Achebe's life and in his writing. What are some examples from *Marriage Is a Private Affair* that show this?**

Follow the steps to write your essay.

Step 1: Work in small groups. Complete the chart to organize ideas from the lecture, reading, and summary.

Differences between Traditional and More Modern Society		
Topics	Traditional (Okeke's generation)	More Modern (Nnaemeka and Nene's generation)
Marriage		
Religion		
Knowledge of traditions		
Women allowed to teach		

Integrated Speaking Task

You have read a text and listened to a lecture about the use of imagination in acting. You have also read synopses of two movies. You will now use the content, vocabulary, and summarizing skills from this unit to give a short talk in answer to this question: **How is imagination useful to an actor preparing for a role? Illustrate your answer with reference to a particular role.**

Follow the steps to prepare your talk.

Step 1: Work with a partner. Think of a film you both know well or think again about the film in the synopsis you read. Then each of you should choose a different character to discuss from that film.

Step 2: Together, discuss and decide how you will each prepare for the role. Use some of the ideas from the lecture and the reading in this unit.

Step 3: Prepare your talk. You can use your notes from the exercises in Before You Speak on page 68. Use the chart to organize your ideas. Remember to think about organizational structure (See Unit 2).

	Your Notes
Actors use their imagination to . . .	
Our film was about . . .	
The characters were . . .	
To prepare for the role ourselves, we discussed . . .	
In the end, we decided to . . .	
To conclude . . .	

MyAcademicConnectionsLab

MyAcademicConnectionsLab, an integral part of the *Academic Connections* series, is an easy-to-use online program that delivers personalized instruction and practice to students and rich resources to teachers.

- Students can access reading and listening selections, do practice activities, and prepare for tests anytime they go online.
- Teachers can take advantage of many resources including online assessments, a flexible gradebook, and tools for monitoring student progress.

The **MyAcademicConnectionsLab** WELCOME page organizes assignments and grades, and facilitates communication between students and teachers. It also allows the teacher to monitor student progress.

For Sections 1–3, MyAcademicConnectionsLab provides Vocabulary Check activities. These activities assess students' knowledge of the vocabulary needed for comprehension of the content and follow up with individualized instruction.

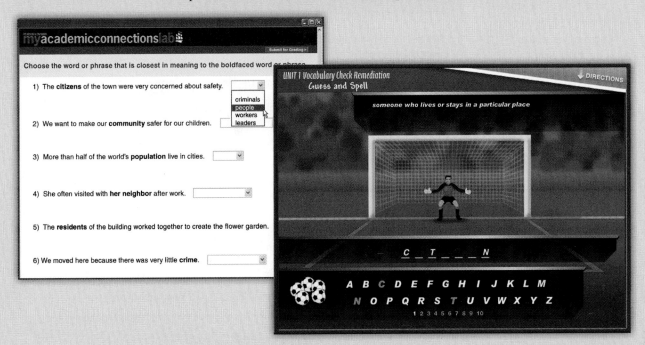

Reading and listening selections from the student book and additional practice activities are available to students online. Students benefit from virtually unlimited practice anywhere, anytime.

- Reading-based activities allow students to further engage with the unit's reading selection. Students practice comprehension, academic skills, grammar, and content vocabulary.

- Listening-based activities allow students to further engage with the unit's listening selection. Students practice comprehension, listening skills, and note-taking skills.

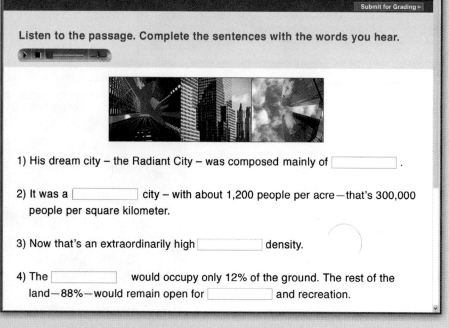

MyAcademicConnectionsLab offers additional activities that support the *Academic Connections* program.

- Fun, interactive games reinforce academic vocabulary and skills.
- Internet-based and discussion-board activities expand students' knowledge of the topic and help them practice new vocabulary.

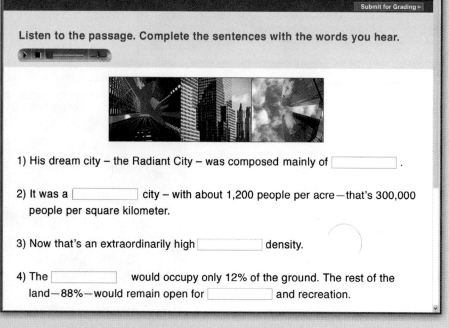

The MyAcademicConnectionsLab ASSESSMENT tools allow instructors to customize and deliver tests online.
- A placement test situates students in the appropriate level (also available in the paper format).
- Pre-course and post-course tests allow teachers to target instruction.
- Section tests monitor student progress.

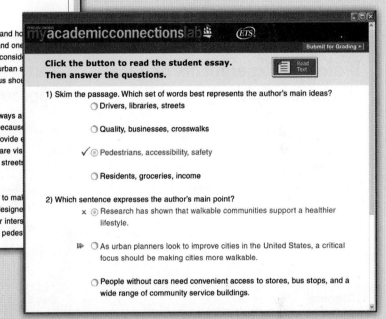

Student: Bob Travertine
Unit: City Planning 201
Date: October 15

Walkable communities

[1] Improving urban transportation involves more than just deciding where and ho build streets and highways. Urban residents need transportation choices, and one available choice should be walking. However, many urban planners do not consid pedestrians as they plan streets and highways and make decisions about urban s As urban planners look to improve cities in the United States, a critical focus shou making cities more walkable.

[2] A walkable community is one that is friendly to pedestrians. It has walkways a most, if not all, of the streets. They are safe for people of all ages to walk because are paved with secure materials and are properly maintained. Walkways provide e access to schools, libraries, bus stops, and stores, and their surroundings are vis appealing. While walkways are wide enough to accommodate pedestrians, streets narrow in order to discourage high-speed driving.

[3] Urban planners should consider a variety of factors when deciding how to mak city more walkable. For example, streets and highways may need to be redesigne order to create space for adding sidewalks, as well as safe crosswalks over inters tions. They can encourage designs which place a physical barrier between pedes

Click the button to read the student essay.
Then answer the questions.

1) Skim the passage. Which set of words best represents the author's main ideas?
- Drivers, libraries, streets
- Quality, businesses, crosswalks
- ✓ Pedestrians, accessibility, safety
- Residents, groceries, income

2) Which sentence expresses the author's main point?
- x Research has shown that walkable communities support a healthier lifestyle.
- ⏩ As urban planners look to improve cities in the United States, a critical focus should be making cities more walkable.
- People without cars need convenient access to stores, bus stops, and a wide range of community service buildings.

Teacher support materials in MyAcademic ConnectionsLab offer tips and suggestions for teaching the *Academic Connections* material and make lesson planning easier.

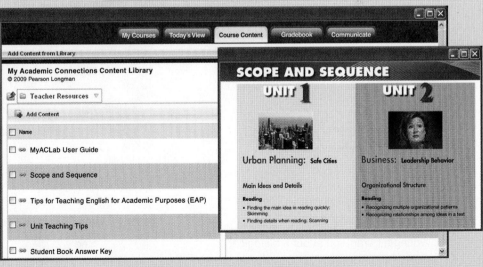

My Courses | Today's View | Course Content | Gradebook | Communicate

Add Content from Library

My Academic Connections Content Library
© 2009 Pearson Longman

Teacher Resources

Add Content

☐ Name
☐ MyACLab User Guide
☐ Scope and Sequence
☐ Tips for Teaching English for Academic Purposes (EAP)
☐ Unit Teaching Tips
☐ Student Book Answer Key

SCOPE AND SEQUENCE

UNIT 1

Urban Planning: Safe Cities

Main Ideas and Details

Reading
- Finding the main idea in reading quickly: Skimming
- Finding details when reading: Scanning

UNIT 2

Business: Leadership Behavior

Organizational Structure

Reading
- Recognizing multiple organizational patterns
- Recognizing relationships among ideas in a text

UNIT 1

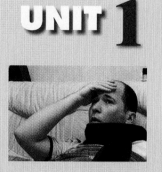

Biology: Experiments and the Common Cold

Main Ideas and Supporting Details

Reading

- Finding main ideas: skimming
- Finding specific information: scanning

Listening

- Getting the gist: understanding a speaker's main ideas
- Listening for supporting details

Writing

- Writing a paragraph
- Recognizing parts of a paragraph

Integrated Writing Task

- Writing a paragraph about a biological experiment

UNIT 2

Marketing: New Ways to Spread the Message

Organizational Structure

Listening

- Recognizing relationships among parts of a lecture
- Organizational structure and note-taking

Reading

- Recognizing organization of written texts
- Recognizing purpose of texts
- Understanding relationships within a reading text

Speaking

- Expressing relationships between ideas

Integrated Speaking Task

- Designing and presenting a stealth or viral marketing campaign

UNIT 3

Astronomy: Collisions from Space

Coherence and Cohesion

Reading
- Recognizing reference in cohesion

Listening
- Recognizing logical connectives in lectures
- Listing ideas

Writing
- Writing cohesive texts

Integrated Writing Task
- Writing a paragraph about the usefulness of research into Near-Earth Objects (NEOs)

UNIT 4

Acting: Imagination

Summarizing

Listening
- Recognizing digressions and asides
- Distinguishing major from minor points

Reading
- Recognizing summary statements and conclusions

Speaking
- Preparing spoken summaries

Integrated Speaking Task
- Summarizing how an actor might use imagination when preparing for a role

UNIT 5

Psychology: Emotions

Synthesizing Information

Reading
- Recognizing abstract ideas and concrete examples

Listening
- Recognizing relationships between ideas from two spoken sources

Writing
- Writing summary statements in paragraphs
- Synthesizing information in writing

Integrated Writing Task
- Writing a paragraph about where emotional responses come from

UNIT 6

Sociology: The Effects of Prosperity

Fact and Opinion

Listening
- Identifying and evaluating information presented to support a position
- Recognizing a speaker's degree of certainty

Reading
- Distinguishing between facts and opinions

Speaking
- Discussing opinions and supporting ideas
- Supporting opinions

Integrated Speaking Task
- Discussing an issue of prosperity versus happiness

UNIT 7

Literature: Chinua Achebe

Purpose

Listening

- Recognizing a speaker's attitude

Reading

- Recognizing multiple purposes in texts

Writing

- Writing introductions and conclusions in essays
- Considering your audience

Integrated Writing Task

- Writing an academic essay about *Marriage Is a Private Affair*

UNIT 8

Earth Science: The Water Cycle

Inference

Reading

- Inferring meaning from context
- Drawing conclusions

Listening

- Inferring the speaker's purpose

Speaking

- Using intonation to convey meaning
- Persuading your audience

Integrated Speaking Task

- Giving a persuasive talk about human intervention in the water cycle

ACKNOWLEDGMENTS

While it is always the case that a book is a team effort, this was especially so with the *Academic Connections* series. I would like to thank all of those at Pearson involved from the initial concept through to editing, production, and marketing. It's impossible to name everyone, but special thanks for level 2 go to John Beaumont, development editor, whose patient guiding hand helped to ensure consistency with the other levels in the series. Those late-night/early-morning phone calls always led to interesting discussions that took far longer than expected!

Of course no author is without influence, and I would also like to acknowledge the numerous friends and colleagues as well as students I have worked with and learned so much from over the years. And on the home front, I extend my special thanks to Chie, whose encouragement, support and above all, patience, have been immensely valuable.

David Hill

The publisher would like to thank the following people.

Matthew Chametzky, R&D Capability Manager at ETS, who coordinated all assessment work for this project, bringing order when chaos seemed imminent.

Terry Cryan, Assessment Specialist at ETS who helped us all better understand (and appreciate) the many differences between testing and teaching.

Kate Kazin, Director of Client Management at ETS, whose clear vision kept the project true to its objective of evidence-based design.

REVIEWERS

For the comments and insights they graciously offered to help shape the direction of *Academic Connections*, the publisher would like to thank the following reviewers and institutions.

Donette Artenie, Georgetown University; **Jennifer Castello**, Cañada College; **Carol A. Chapelle**, Iowa State University; **JoAnn (Jodi) Crandall**, University of Maryland; **Wendy Crockett**, J. W. North High School; **Lois Darlington**, Columbia University; **Christopher Davis**, John Jay College; **Robert Dickey**, Gyeongju University, Gyeongju, Korea; **Deborah B. Gordon**, Santa Barbara City College; **Mike Hammond**, University of California, San Diego; **Ian Hosack**, Ritsumeikan University, Kyoto; **Sylvie Huneault-Schultze**, Fresno City College; **Barbara Inerfeld**, Rutgers University; **Joan Jamieson**, Northern Arizona University; **Scott Jenison**, Antelope Valley College; **Mandy Kama**, Georgetown University; **Dr. Jose Lai**, The Chinese University of Hong Kong; **Rama Mathew**, Delhi University, Delhi, India; **Mitchell Mirkin**, Baltimore City Community College; **Carla Billings Nyssen**, California State University, Long Beach; **Yannick O'Neill**, Gyeongnam Education Board, Changwon, South Korea; **Gretchen Owens**, San Francisco State University; **Angela Parrino**, Hunter College; **Sarah C. Saxer**, Howard Community College; **Diane Schmitt**, Nottingham Trent University, Nottingham U.K.; **Gail Schmitt**, Montgomery College; **Fred Servito**, University of Washington; **Janet Shanks Van Suntum**, Fordham University, Pace University; **Karen Shimoda**, Freelance ESL Development Editor; **Dean E. Stafford**, Sanho Elementary School, Mason, South Korea; **Fredricka L. Stoller**, Northern Arizona University; **Richmond Stroupe**, Soka University, Tokyo; **Jessica Williams**, University of Illinois; **Kirsten Windahl**, Cuyahoga Community College

UNIT
1

Biology
Experiments and the Common Cold

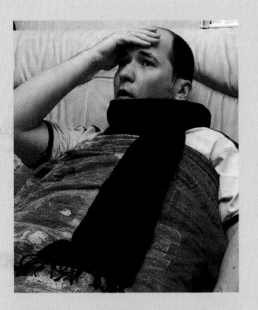

Unit Description

Content: This course is designed to familiarize the student with concepts in biology and biological research.

Skills: Main Ideas and Supporting Details

- Finding main ideas: skimming
- Finding specific information: scanning
- Getting the gist: Understanding a speaker's main ideas
- Listening for supporting details
- Writing a paragraph
- Recognizing parts of a paragraph

Unit Requirements

Reading: "Hypotheses" (an excerpt from a biology textbook)

Lecture: "The Experimental Method"

Listening: "Common Myths about Colds" (a radio broadcast)

Integrated Writing Task: Writing a paragraph about a biological experiment

Assignments: www.MyAcademicConnectionsLab.com

Preview

For online assignments, go to

Previewing the Academic Content

There is one thing common to all people around the world: we will all get many colds during our lives. The common cold is perhaps the most common illness in the world. So, why isn't there any good medicine for it? How can scientists look for a way to help people with a cold?

In this unit, you will look at how biologists can use experiments to learn about illnesses. We will use the common cold as an example. You will also read and hear some information about the common cold.

1. *Look at the ad. What do you think is wrong with the people in the picture?*

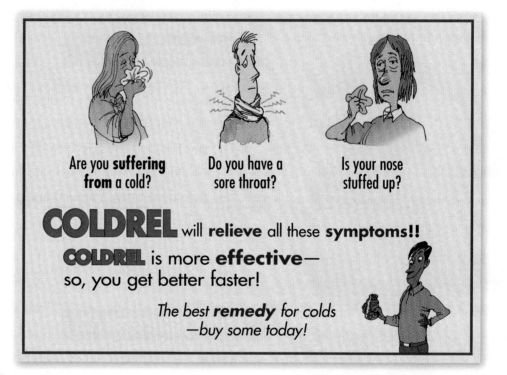

Are you **suffering from** a cold?

Do you have a sore throat?

Is your nose stuffed up?

COLDREL will **relieve** all these **symptoms!!**

COLDREL is more **effective**— so, you get better faster!

*The best **remedy** for colds —buy some today!*

Key Words

effective
relieve
remedy
suffering from
symptom

2. *Find the key words in the ad and guess their meaning from context. Then write each key word next to its definition. Discuss your answers with a partner.*

1. _____*symptom*_____ a problem with your body that shows you are ill

2. _____ make something better

3. _____ something, such as a medicine, that makes you a little better

4. _____ works very well

5. _____ having (an illness)

Do you believe the ad? Why or why not?

3. Work with a partner. List as many symptoms of a cold and remedies as you can. Start with the symptoms and remedies in the ad on page 2.

Symptoms	Remedies
sore throat	

4. Work in small groups. Discuss a time when you suffered from a cold. Answer the questions.

1. What were your symptoms?

2. What remedies did you try?

3. Did the remedies relieve your symptoms?

In this unit, you will learn to find and use main ideas and details.

Previewing the Academic Skills Focus

Main Ideas and Supporting Details

The **main idea** is the writer or speaker's most important idea or point. A **supporting detail** is a piece of information that gives more information about the main idea.

It is very useful to understand main ideas and supporting details. In reading and listening, thinking about them can help you to understand more easily. You can make your writing clear by following conventions[1] about main ideas and details, which you will learn in this unit.

In writing, main ideas and supporting details usually go together in the same paragraph. A paragraph expresses or develops one main idea with supporting details. There is usually a blank line separating each paragraph, but sometimes the first word of a paragraph is indented instead—that is, the first line of the paragraph starts with some space before it.

1. Work with a partner. Where do you expect the main idea to be? Check (✔) all answers that you think may apply.

❑ in the title

❑ at the beginning of the paragraph

❑ in the middle of the paragraph

❑ at the end of the paragraph

❑ repeated throughout the paragraph

---

[1] **conventions** *n, pl* standard ways of doing things

2. *Read the paragraph from a biology textbook. Then answer the questions. Compare your answers with a partner's.*

Are we all scientists?

Most people use a scientific process in their everyday lives to solve problems, such as curing an illness. If you catch a cold and ask your friends and family how to relieve the symptoms, you will hear the usual advice: Take a lot of vitamin C, use echinacea, keep warm, wear your hat and a warm coat outside, get plently of sleep, and take two aspirin and visit the doctor in the morning. What should you do? Most people follow the advice that makes the most sense to them, and if they find that they still feel ill, they try another remedy. This is the kind of science that most of us use daily. We see a problem, think of a few ways to solve it, and choose the way we think will work. If our first choice does not work, we move to our second choice and try again. Thus, science and everyday life are not really very different.

Source: Adapted from Belk, C., & Borden Maier, V. (2007). *Biology: Science for life with physiology* (2nd ed.). San Francisco: Pearson Benjamin Cummings

1. What is the main idea of the paragraph?

   _____

2. Which of these strategies did you use to find the main idea?
   - ❏ I read the title.
   - ❏ I focused on the beginning and end of the paragraph.
   - ❏ I looked for repeated words and ideas.
   - ❏ I tried other strategies.

3. *Discuss your answers with a partner.*

1. Which of the strategies was most helpful for finding the main idea here?
2. Which strategies have you used before?
3. Which strategy would you use first with any text?

2 Building Academic Reading Skills

In this section, you will practice identifying main ideas and specific details in a text.
For online assignments, go to

Before You Read

*Work with a partner. Look at the flowchart on the next page. Then read the statements. Decide if they are true or false. Write **T** (true) or **F** (false). If the statement is false, explain why.*

___T___ 1. The hypothesis in this flowchart is "Taking vitamin C helps your body fight off colds."

_____ 2. Before the experiment, the scientists are sure that the hypothesis is the correct explanation.

_____ 3. Group A takes extra vitamin C.

_____ 4. If group B catches fewer colds than group A, the biologists will keep the hypothesis.

_____ 5. If the biologists keep the hypothesis, they will stop testing.

explain *v* to say how or why something happens; **explanation** *n*

predict *v* to say something will happen before it actually happens; **prediction** *n*

prevent *v* to stop something from happening; **prevention** *n*

research *v* to try to discover new things; **research** *n*; **researcher** *n*

reject *v* to decide not to use or agree with something; **rejection** *n*

support *v* to show that something is correct or that it might be correct; **support** *n*

Figure 1.1: The Experimental Method
How to Test Hypotheses

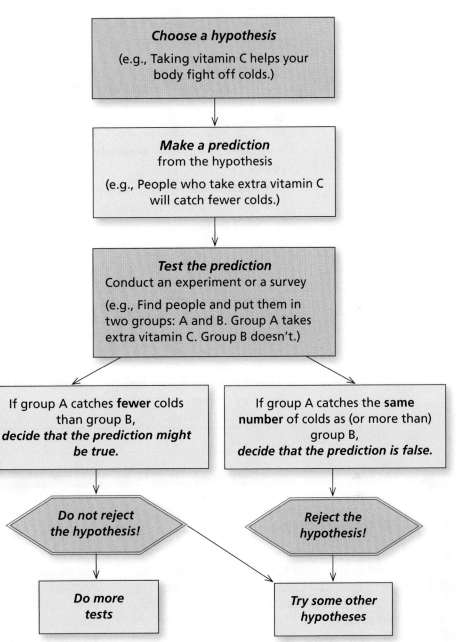

Source: Adapted from Belk, C., & Borden Maier, V. (2007). *Biology: Science for life with physiology* (2nd ed.). San Francisco: Pearson Benjamin Cummings.

Global Reading

1. Work with a partner. Look at the strategies for skimming in the box. Compare them with the strategies for finding the main idea you checked on page 4. Tell your partner which strategies are the same.

Finding Main Ideas: Skimming

Skimming means reading quickly to understand the general meaning of a whole text. It can help you find the main ideas of paragraphs.

Here are some strategies to use when skimming.

Do:
- Read the title, headings, and subheadings of a text.
- Look out for **bold**, *italicized*, or underlined words.
- Read the first and last parts of each paragraph.

Don't:
- Don't use a dictionary.
- Don't think about the meaning of difficult words. You can do that later.
- Don't read every word.

It is a good idea to skim every text before you read it in detail. This will help you know what the text is about and where each main idea is.

2. Skim the excerpt from a biology textbook. What is the main idea? Then compare answers with a classmate's.

_____

_____

Hypotheses

1   The hypothesis is central to each experiment, so we need to know what hypotheses are and where they come from. As we saw earlier, our friends and family often give advice about avoiding colds (for example, the advice to wear a hat or take vitamin C). This kind of advice comes in part from what they know about how our bodies fight colds. Ideas about "how things work" are called hypotheses. Or, in other words, a hypothesis is an idea to explain one or more things we observe. All of us form hypotheses about why things happen. These come from our understanding of the world. When a mother tells her children to wear warm clothes, her advice comes from the following hypothesis: Getting cold makes it easier to catch a cold. Hypotheses in biology come from knowing how the body and other biological systems work, our experiences in similar situations, what we know about other scientific research, and logical thinking. Our creative minds also help.

2   A scientific hypothesis must be falsifiable. That is, you must be able to imagine a way to show that it is false, such as by giving an example showing that it is wrong. For instance, think about the hypothesis that you get more colds in cold weather. We could look at one group of people who spend time in cold temperatures and another group who stay in warm temperatures. If both groups get the same number of colds, the hypothesis might be false. So, this hypothesis is falsifiable. Of

course, scientists do not show every hypothesis to be false—the important point is that proving them false is possible. This is why personal opinions, such as "It is wrong to cheat on exams," are not scientific—each person has a different idea about right and wrong. It is not possible to falsify personal opinions.

3 Hypotheses must also be testable. This means it must be possible to check them by seeing or measuring things. Not all hypotheses are testable. For example, we cannot test hypotheses that need a supernatural[1] force. If something is supernatural, it does not follow the laws of nature, and we cannot predict its behavior: we can't measure anything about it.

4 An example of a common hypothesis about colds is that taking extra vitamin C prevents colds. This is very easy to believe, especially when you think about the following generally known facts:

- Fruits and vegetables have a lot of vitamin C.

- People who eat a lot of fruits and vegetables are often healthier than people who eat less of these foods.

- Vitamin C is known to help with sore throats and nose irritation.

Given these facts, we can state the following falsifiable and testable hypothesis: Taking vitamin C lowers the chance of catching a cold.

5 However, sometimes a hypothesis might seem to be true after the first test, but scientists reject it later after a different test. This is what actually happened with the hypothesis that taking vitamin C keeps colds away. A 1970 book by the Nobel Prize winner Linus Pauling agreed with this hypothesis. Since then, however, repeated, careful tests have failed to support it. Also, people found that the results in Pauling's book may have had other explanations. Today, most common cold researchers do not agree with this hypothesis.

---

[1] **supernatural** *adj* impossible to explain by science or other natural causes; things like ghosts, gods, and magic are supernatural.

Source: Adapted from Belk, C., & Borden Maier, V. (2007). *Biology: Science for life with physiology* (2nd ed.). San Francisco: Pearson Benjamin Cummings.

3. Skim the text again. Write the main idea of each paragraph in your own words.

Paragraph 1: *What hypotheses are* _____

Paragraph 2: _____

Paragraph 3: _____

Paragraph 4: _____

Paragraph 5: _____

4. Read the questions. Using your responses in Exercise 3, write the number of the paragraph where you can find the answers to the questions. Do not look back at the reading.

_____ a. What is the definition of *hypothesis?*

_____ b. What does *testable* mean?

_____ c. What is one kind of hypothesis that cannot be tested?

_____ d. What does *falsifiable* mean?

_____ e. What is one kind of statement that cannot be falsified?

_____ f. Why is it often necessary to test a hypothesis more than once?

5. Answer the questions in Exercise 4 by reading in detail only the paragraphs you chose. Then compare your answers with a partner's.

a. _____

b. _____

c. _____

d. _____

e. _____

f. _____

_____

Focused Reading

1. Read paragraphs 2 and 3 on pages 6–7. Find examples of the three elements listed. Underline them. Then compare your answers with a partner's.
- two definitions
- three examples
- an explanation (not just a description)

2. Which expressions in the reading introduce a definition, an example, or an explanation? Work with your partner to complete the chart.

Type of Supporting Idea	Phrases Introducing Supporting Ideas
Definition	*This means*
Example	
Explanation	

Scanning can also help you find ideas quickly. It is different from skimming because you are looking for details, not a main idea.

Scanning means reading quickly to find specific information such as words, ideas, numbers, names, places, and dates. Specific information is often found in the supporting details. These could be definitions, examples, or explanations.

As with skimming, when scanning, do not read every word.

Here are some strategies to help you scan:

- Look for capital letters if you are looking for a place or a name.
- Look for numbers if you are looking for answers to questions about dates, times, etc.
- Find a key word in the question, or a word with the same meaning, and search for it.

3. Work with a partner. Look at each question in the chart. Think about what you will scan for to find the answers: capital letter, number, or key word. Check (✓) all that apply. If you check key word, also underline the key word in the question. Do not look back at the reading.

	What will you scan for?		
	Capital Letter	Number	Key Word
1. What is a hypothesis that a mother might use?			
2. What kinds of food have a lot of vitamin C?			
3. Who wrote a book about vitamin C and colds?			
4. When did he write it?			
5. What famous prize did he win?			
6. Do scientists agree with the book now?			

4. Scan the reading on pages 6–7 and write the answers to the questions in the chart. Then compare your answers with a classmate's.

1. _____

2. _____

3. _____

4. _____

5. _____

6. _____

Unit 1 ■ Experiments and the Common Cold   **9**

5. Work in small groups. Look at the example hypotheses in the chart. Discuss whether they are good or not. Check (✓) one column for each.

Example Hypothesis	Rejected Because Not Falsifiable	Rejected Because Not Testable	Not Rejected
1. People cannot think as clearly when they have a cold.			
2. You should not go to work or school when you have a cold.			
3. Getting a cold is a sign that ghosts or spirits are unhappy with you.			
4. Thousands of years ago, people experienced the same cold symptoms as they do now.			

Work with someone from another group. Explain the reasons for your group's answers to your new partner. Listen to your partner's reasons.

6. Work with a new partner. Discuss your reactions to the reading.

1. What new information did you learn from this text?

2. Which piece of information was most interesting to you? Why?

3. Where else might you read or hear about hypotheses, outside of biology lessons?

Checkpoint 1   PEARSON LONGMAN myacademicconnectionslab

Before You Listen

Work with a partner. Look at the picture of a cold medicine. Then discuss the questions.

1. How might this product be useful?

2. Have you seen any similar products? How well do they work?

3. Do you think the product in the picture is effective? Explain.

Natulief
The natural way to prevent colds.

Hundreds of years ago, the people of the outback of Australia used the leaves of a special type of eucalyptus tree to treat colds. The secret of this cure was thought to be lost.... until now. Our researchers have found the secret ingredient, and refined it. Now, it is available for YOU. Natulief Eucalyptus Oil will help you recover from colds faster!

3
Building Academic Listening Skills

In this section, you will practice identifying main ideas and details in lectures.
For online assignments, go to

PEARSON LONGMAN myacademicconnectionslab

Global Listening

Getting the **gist** means listening for the main ideas and general information. Listening for the gist is similar to skimming in reading. When listening for the gist, do not pay attention to details.

Here are some strategies for getting the gist in a lecture:

- Before a lecture, read any information you have about the course: Sometimes students get a course summary, syllabus, or outline at the beginning of the course.
- Listen carefully to the beginning of a lecture. Lecturers often give the main ideas in the intrduction.
- Listen for signals, such as:

    I'm going to talk about . . .

    Now, let's move on to . . .

- Listen carefully to the end of the lecture. There is often a summary of the main ideas there.

1. *To prepare for the lecture, read part of the course outline posted by the professor online. Then answer the question.*

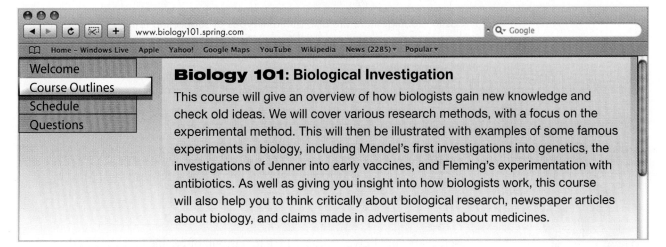

www.biology101.spring.com

Welcome
Course Outlines
Schedule
Questions

Biology 101: Biological Investigation

This course will give an overview of how biologists gain new knowledge and check old ideas. We will cover various research methods, with a focus on the experimental method. This will then be illustrated with examples of some famous experiments in biology, including Mendel's first investigations into genetics, the investigations of Jenner into early vaccines, and Fleming's experimentation with antibiotics. As well as giving you insight into how biologists work, this course will also help you to think critically about biological research, newspaper articles about biology, and claims made in advertisements about medicines.

What do you already know about this topic? Tell your partner.

2. *Listen to the first part of the lecture. Check (✓) the ideas that you hear.*

1. Controls/controlled experiments ☐
2. Placebos ☐
3. Deaf experiments ☐
4. Blind experiments ☐
5. Double-blind experiments ☐
6. Testable hypotheses ☐

Key Words

conduct *v* to do something in an organized way in order to get information

treatment *n* a method that is used to cure a sickness

3. 🎧 *Listen to the whole lecture. Which main idea from Exercise 2 is introduced after these expressions? Write the number of the idea on the line.*

1. First of all, . . . _____

2. . . . and it's an important answer . . . _____

3. . . . our next idea . . . _____

4. . . . this brings us to the next point . . . _____

4. *What is the connection between the introduction and the body of the lecture?*

5. *Using your answers in Exercises 2 and 3, as well as the information in the skill box, what are the four main ideas of the lecture?*

_____

_____

_____

_____

Focused Listening

Listening for Supporting Details

Just as in reading, there are also different types of supporting ideas in listening such as examples, definitions, and explanations. In order to notice these details, listen for expressions that introduce them, such as: *for example, for instance, in other words, what is . . .?*

1. 🎧 *Read the statements. Then listen to the lecture again. As you listen, complete each statement.*

1. First of all, controlled experiments. The best way to explain these is with _____, which we'll look at over the next few minutes. Maybe some of you . . .

2. Our example experiment will help us find out. _____, scientists could give echinacea tea to a group of people and see whether their colds got better more quickly than normal.

3. Or _____, the only difference between the experimental group and the control group is the reason for the experiment—the treatment.

4. What is a placebo? _____ does nothing! It has no effect. But it looks just like the medicine, the treatment.

5. In our echinacea experiment, _____, the placebo looks just like echinacea tea.

6. When the research assistants and the participants are all blinded, _____ "double-blind" experiment.

2. Look at the statements in Exercise 1. Which statements are examples, and which are definitions? Write the number.

Examples: _1,_____

Definitions: _____

3. Look at the expressions you wrote in Exercise 1. Which expressions indicate an example, and which indicate a definition?

Examples: _an example,_____

Definitions: _____

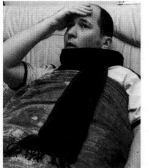

4. 🎧 Read the summary. Then listen to the lecture again and complete the statements. Compare your answers with a partner's.

Echinacea tea is used in the example of a controlled experiment. It is a kind of herbal tea made from parts of the echinacea (1) _____. In the example, scientists give echinacea to a group of people and see whether their colds get (2) _____ more (3) _____. A control group is also used. The control group is the (4) _____ as the experimental group, but it does not get the (5) _____, in this case the echinacea. Instead, the people get a placebo, which does (6) _____; it has (7) _____ effect. Thus, this is a blind experiment: In a blind experiment, people (8) _____ what they're taking or which group they are in.

5. Circle the best answer to complete each statement. Then compare your answers with a partner's. What are the reasons for your answers?

1. The speaker's tone[1] indicates she _____ advertisements about echinacea.
   a. hates
   b. never believes
   c. doesn't always believe
   d. believes

2. The hypothesis in the echinacea tea experiment is that echinacea tea _____.
   a. helps to prevent colds
   b. helps you get better from colds
   c. is better than vitamin C
   d. is an herbal tea

3. If the experimental group's colds are shorter than the control group's, this shows that echinacea tea _____.
   a. might be a good cold remedy
   b. might be a bad cold remedy
   c. helps to prevent colds
   d. is the best cold remedy you can take

---

[1] **tone** *n* the feeling or attitude in a speaker's voice

4. If the experimental group took vitamin C tablets, not echinacea, the placebo would be _____.
   a. tablets that say "echinacea" on the package
   b. tea containing vitamin C
   c. tablets containing vitamin C
   d. tablets that look like common vitamin C tablets

5. If the experiment is blind, _____.
   a. the people know which group they are in
   b. the people cannot see what they are taking
   c. the people do not know if they are taking echinacea tea
   d. the placebo tea is clearly different from the echinacea tea

6. Work in two groups, Group A and Group B. Group A will design a controlled experiment to test whether Natulief helps you get better more quickly (look at the picture on page 10). Group B will design a controlled experiment to test whether getting more sleep will help you get better faster from colds (getting more sleep was mentioned in the paragraph on page 4). Use the chart to organize your ideas. Then follow the steps to complete the task.

	Group _____
Give a falsifiable, testable hypothesis.	
What will the experimental group do?	
What will the control group do?	
Will there be a placebo? If so, what is it? If not, why not?	
Can you make the experiment blind? If so, how? If not, why not?	

1. Work with a partner from your group. Take turns explaining the experiment to each other.

2. Work with a person from the opposite group. Take turns explaining your experiment to each other.

3. Discuss the differences between your experiments.

Checkpoint 2   PEARSON LONGMAN myacademicconnectionslab

4

Building Academic Writing Skills

In this section, you will practice recognizing parts of a paragraph. Then you will write a paragraph about whether people should take vitamin C to prevent colds using information from the reading and the lecture in this unit and from a radio talk you will hear. For online assignments, go to

myacademicconnectionslab

Before You Write

1. *Read the paragraph from a biology textbook. Then complete the tasks.*

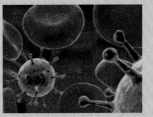

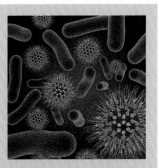

Microorganisms are the cause of many illnesses. Two major types of microorganisms are *bacteria* and *viruses*. Both are microscopic; that is, people can only see them with a microscope.[1] However, most bacteria are much bigger than most viruses. Bacteria can reproduce[2] by themselves, but viruses must infect a plant or animal to reproduce. Bacteria can usually be killed by a type of medicine called "antibiotics." However, antibiotics do not kill viruses; in fact, very few medicines kill viruses. The common cold is an example of an illness caused by a virus. Many kinds of food poisoning are caused by bacteria.

[1] **microscope** *n* 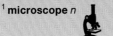   [2] **reproduce** *v* make new copies of oneself. When humans reproduce, they have babies.

1. Underline the main idea of the paragraph.

2. Look again at the texts on page 4 and pages 6–7. How do you know when a paragraph begins and ends?

Writing a Paragraph

When writing paragraphs, remember to make sure each paragraph:
- has one and only one main idea
- is clearly separated from other paragraphs, either by indenting (as on page 4) or by leaving a blank line before and after it (as on pages 6–7)

2. *Work with a partner. Look at the two groups of sentences. Discuss what you need to do to make each group into a paragraph. Write the paragraphs in correct form on a separate piece of paper.*

Group 1

Many people wonder why it is so difficult to find a medicine to cure colds.
The reason is that colds are caused by viruses, not by bacteria.
There are many kinds of medicine that kill bacteria.
These are called "antibiotics."
Antibiotics don't kill viruses.
Scientists have only found a few safe medicines to kill viruses, and none of them kill cold viruses.

Group 2

So, how do people get better from colds? The answer is that the body has a system that can kill many kinds of viruses. This is called the "immune system." Colds are very bad for the economy. Most people take time off from work every year because of a cold, so they make less money for their company. If people go to work with a cold, they cannot work so hard. They may also pass their cold to someone else. Thus, the result is the same or worse than taking time off.

Focused Writing

Recognizing Parts of a Paragraph

Most paragraphs have two main parts. They have a **topic sentence** that gives the main idea of a paragraph. It is usually, but not always, the first sentence of a paragraph.

The sentences after the topic sentence give **supporting details**. As we saw before, supporting details can be explanations, examples, or definitions. They can also be any other information that helps us understand, know more about, or believe the main ideas.

1. Look back at the reading on pages 6–7. Underline the topic sentences in paragraphs 2, 3, 4, and 5. Which sentences did you read when you skimmed?

2. Read the paragraphs. Underline the topic sentence in each.

Paragraph 1

Chicken soup has been a common North American remedy for colds for many years—but does it work? Scientists have carried out experiments to investigate exactly that question. They found that, generally, it does work! Then other researchers at the University of Nebraska compared homemade chicken soup with the types that supermarkets sell in cans. The result was that most types of canned chicken soup were just as effective as homemade chicken soup.

Paragraph 2

There are many kinds of viruses that cause the cold. The most common is the rhinovirus, a type of picornavirus. Other examples of cold viruses are coronaviruses, human parainfluenza viruses, adenoviruses, and enteroviruses.

Paragraph 3

Does echinacea stop the common cold? There have been several studies on this. Some show that there is no effect and others show a large effect. In 2007, Dr. Craig Coleman at the University of Connecticut looked at 14 different studies. After analysis, the results were very surprising. People taking echinacea got 58 percent fewer colds, and these colds lasted one and a half days shorter than with those who did not take it.

Paragraph 4

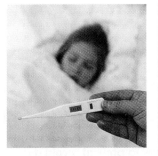

The immune system is the body's natural defense system. It helps the body kill infections[1] from viruses and bacteria, such as colds and food poisoning. There are several different parts to the immune system. One part is the *innate immune system*. This gives a general response to the infection, the same for any infection, such as fever. The other is the *adaptive immune system*. This is different from the innate immune system because it attacks each infection differently.

_____

[1] **infection** *n* a disease caused by something, usually a virus or bacteria, entering your body

3. *What type of supporting detail is used? Check (✓) the correct column or columns in the chart. Not every paragraph uses these types.*

	Example(s)	Definition(s)	Explanation(s)
Paragraph 1			
Paragraph 2			
Paragraph 3			
Paragraph 4			

4. ⌒ *To prepare for writing practice, listen to the announcer of a radio program talk about colds. As you listen, take notes in your notebook.*

5. *Work with a partner. Use your notes to complete the chart.*

The announcer's . . .	
Main idea	
Supporting details	

6. *Write a paragraph to answer this question:* **Which ways to prevent a cold do and do not work?** *Follow the steps.*

Step 1: Look at the chart you completed in Exercise 5. Mark the supporting details that are about the question.

Step 2: Write a topic sentence.

Step 3: Write the supporting details.

Step 4: Check that your paragraph has:

❏ a clear topic sentence giving the main idea

❏ clear supporting ideas that help the reader know more about the main idea

❏ correct formatting

Step 5: Revise your paragraph if necessary.

Integrated Writing Task

You have listened to a lecture and a radio talk, and read texts about scientific experiments and the common cold. You will now use your knowledge of the content, vocabulary, and paragraph writing to write a paragraph in response to this question: **How can biologists find out whether vitamin C prevents colds?**

Follow the steps to write your paragraph.

Step 1: Make notes in the chart on the next page of ideas from the reading, lecture, and radio talk that might be useful for your paragraph. Compare your notes with a partner's. Then mark the ideas you think are most useful for your paragraph.

From the reading	What do we need to know about hypotheses to design the experiment?	
From the lecture	What features do controlled experiments have?	
From the radio segment	How did the experiment on the radio work?	

Step 2: Write your paragraph.
- Choose the main idea.
- Write the topic sentence.
- Write the supporting details, using the chart to help you.

Step 3: Work with a partner. Exchange your paragraphs. Comment on each other's paragraphs. Use the checklist.

Does the paragraph have. . .	Yes
a topic sentence that gives the main idea?	
a clear main idea?	
details that support the main idea?	
a clear formatting?	

Step 4: Based on your discussion with your partner, write a final draft of your paragraph and give it to your teacher.

Marketing

New Ways to Spread the Message

Unit Description

Content: This course is designed to familiarize the student with concepts in marketing and advertising.

Skills: Organizational Structure
- Recognizing relationships among parts of a lecture
- Organizational structure and note-taking
- Recognizing organization of written texts
- Recognizing purpose of texts
- Understanding relationships within a reading text
- Expressing relationships between ideas

Unit Requirements

Lecture: "New Ways in Advertising"

Reading: "Advertising" (an excerpt from a marketing textbook)

Listening: "Advice from the Professor"

Integrated Speaking Task: Designing and presenting a stealth or viral marketing campaign

Assignments: www.MyAcademicConnectionsLab.com

Previewing the Academic Content

Companies want to sell their products, but to sell as many as possible, they have to tell many people about the products. Advertising helps to do this. However, advertising can also have its problems. One is that people see so many advertisements nowadays that they stop noticing them. Advertisers have some very interesting ways to overcome this problem. In this unit we will look at some of the methods advertisers use and also look at some of the goals of advertising.

Key Words

ad *n* short for advertisement, a picture, short film etc., that a company uses to tell people about their product; **advertise** *v*, **advertising** *n*

goal *n* something you want to do or get; the reason for doing something

media *n, pl.* the ways that people get information (e.g., TV, newspapers, and the Internet); **medium** *n, sing.*

notice *v* to see or hear something

product *n* something that companies make and sell

1. *Work in small groups. Think of an ad you have seen or heard and describe it to your group using the questions in the chart. Take notes in the chart about the other students' answers.*

	Your Ad	Student 2's Ad	Student 3's Ad
What was the type of media?			
What product did it advertise?			
Describe the ad.			

	Your Ad	Student 2's Ad	Student 3's Ad
What did you learn about the product?			
What is your opinion of the ad? Explain.			

2. *Work in small groups. Choose one of the ads from the chart. Then answer the questions. Circle the best answers and add some of your own. More than one answer is possible.*

1. What audience was the ad for?
   - teenagers
   - adults with children
   - young adult females
   - _____
   - _____

2. How do you know the ad was for this audience?
   - The product was for these people.
   - The ad was in a magazine these people often read.
   - The ad was on TV at a time these people often watch TV.
   - _____
   - _____

3. What was the goal of the ad?
   - to give information about a new product
   - to compare one product with another and show that it's better
   - to keep a well-known product in your mind
   - _____
   - _____

This unit will help you to see and follow the organizational structure of lectures, essays, and other academic texts.

Previewing the Academic Skills Focus

Organizational Structure

Organizational structure is the pattern of ideas across the text or lecture. Many lectures, essays, and academic textbook sections in English follow the same basic structure:

- The **introduction** gives the main idea of the text. It opens the topic with important general information (**the general statement**). The introduction also gives the main idea(s) of the text (the **scope**). The general statement and scope can be one or more sentences in length.
- The **body** gives more specific information about the main idea. It gives explanations, examples, reasons, effects, etc.
- The **conclusion** returns to the main idea presented in the introduction and closes the topic.

The introduction and the conclusion are usually short. The body is the longer, main part of the text.

Recognizing the organizational structure can help you to follow the main ideas throughout a lecture or reading. When you give talks or write essays, organizing your ideas into a structure can help people understand you clearly.

1. *Read the introduction to a chapter in a marketing textbook. Underline the general statement once and the scope twice.*

IN THIS CHAPTER, we'll look at how to get advertisements into the right place at the right time for the right people to see them. First, we'll look at things like the type of medium—which kind of magazine or TV show is the best place to advertise a particular product. After that, we'll move on to the timing of ad campaigns. This includes the time of day in the case of radio, TV, and the Internet, and also the time of the week and the season of the year. We'll finish by looking at new ways that people get their message to their customers. We'll see that clever companies do more than use just traditional advertising.

2. *Work with a partner. Discuss the questions.*

1. What main ideas will come up later in the unit?

2. Which ideas might the conclusion mention?

2

Building Academic Listening Skills

In this section, you will practice recognizing the relationships among various parts of a lecture. You will also practice following organizational structure in lectures and practice taking notes.
For online assignments, go to

PEARSON LONGMAN
myacademicconnectionslab

Before You Listen

1. *Think about something you bought, either an electronic item or an item of clothing. Work in groups. Answer the questions.*

1. What was it?

2. What brand was it?

3. Was it a brand name item?

4. How did you find out about the product? Check the boxes.
   ❏ from friends
   ❏ from family
   ❏ advertising
   ❏ other: _____

5. Which of the items in question 4 influenced your decision to buy? Which was the biggest influence?

2. *Compare your answers to questions 4 and 5 in Exercise 1 to those of other students in your class. Which was the most popular way to find out about a product? Which usually had the biggest influence?*

Global Listening

Key Words

brand *n* the name of any company or product
brand name *n* the name of a well-known brand;
brand-name *adj*
influence *v* to change the way people think;
influence *n*
strategy *n* a careful plan or method to complete something

Recognizing Relationships among Parts of a Lecture

We saw earlier that the main ideas are mentioned in the scope, then again (with supporting details) in the body, and again in the conclusion. But how can you recognize which idea is a main idea?

The answer is that speakers usually use special words and expressions called **signals** to tell listeners what the main ideas are. For example, a lecturer might say in the scope:

First, we'll look at marketing brand-name products. Then, we'll move on to other kinds of products.

The signals in this example are *First, we'll look at . . .* and *Then, we'll move on to . . .*

Similar signals are used in the body of the lecture to introduce each main idea.

Also, these signals introduce the conclusion: *To conclude . . .* and *In summary . . .*

Within the signals are often words or expressions called **logical connectives**. These tell you the relationships between ideas. For example, *however* shows that the next idea is different from the one before. *Because* shows that the next idea is a reason.

If you listen carefully for the signals and logical connectives, the structure of the text will be clear.

1. 🎧 *Listen to the introduction of the lecture. Then answer the questions.*

1. What is the general statement about? Circle the best answer.
   a. a new idea for advertisers
   b. a problem for advertisers
   c. a problem for ordinary people

2. What ideas are presented in the scope? Draw a line connecting the expressions from the scope to the main ideas they introduce.

Expression	Main Idea in the Scope
Today, we'll look at	viral marketing
First,	new marketing strategies
then	stealth marketing

2. 🎧 *Listen to the body of the lecture. Then complete the statements.*

1. _____ introduces the first main idea.
   a. So, first of all . . .
   b. Let's start with . . .

2. The first main idea is _____.

3. _____ introduces the next main idea.
   a. Next, I'll talk about . . .
   b. The next type of marketing to talk about is . . .

4. The next main idea is _____.

3. 🎧 *Listen to the conclusion of the lecture. Then answer the questions.*

1. Which expression introduces the conclusion? Circle the correct answer.
   a. So, to conclude . . .
   b. So there we have it

2. Which main ideas are mentioned in the conclusion?

   _____

3. According to the lecturer, how do companies feel about viral marketing and stealth marketing? Circle the correct answer.
   a. They are worried about these strategies.
   b. They are excited about these strategies.
   c. They are no longer interested in these strategies.

4. Check (✓) the choice that best summarizes the organizational structure of the lecture.

❏ 1. **Introduce a process**
    Step 1 in the process
    Step 2 in the process
    Conclusion

❏ 2. **Introduce an opinion**
    Reason 1 for the opinion
    Reason 2 for the opinion
    Conclusion

❏ 3. **Introduce ideas to be explained**
    Explanation of idea 1
    Explanation of idea 2
    Conclusion

Focused Listening

Organizational Structure and Note-taking

Note-taking is important at the university level because it can help you remember what the professors said in lectures.

Understanding how lectures are organized can help you with note-taking. One way to take notes is to use a chart.

Introduction General statement Scope	
Main idea 1	Supporting details about main idea 1
Main idea 2	Supporting details about main idea 2
Main idea 3	Supporting details about main idea 3
Conclusion	

1. ⌒ Review organizational structure on page 24. Then listen to the lecture and complete the outline. Compare your notes with a partner's.

INTRODUCTION **Ideas in the general statement:**	
Main ideas in the scope: *New marketing strategies—stealth and viral marketing*	
Main idea 1:	**Definition:** **Advertising medium:** **Examples:** **Advantages:**

(continued on next page)

Main idea 2:	Definition:
	Examples:
	Advantages:
	Dangers:
Conclusion:	

2. *Work with a partner. Use your notes to complete the sentences.*

1. In both viral marketing and stealth marketing:
   - The message has to be interesting so that _____.
   - The advertising medium is _____.
   - Word-of-mouth is effective because _____.
   - Costs are low because _____.

2. In the example of viral marketing, controlling the number of invitations made people feel _____.

3. In the example of stealth marketing, the teenagers don't say

   _____

4. In viral marketing, everyone knows that the marketers are selling a product. When people don't know this, it is called _____.

3. *Work in small groups. Discuss your answers to the questions.*

1. What is an example of a viral marketing or stealth marketing campaign you have seen? Explain.

2. Do you think viral marketing is honest or dishonest? Explain. How about stealth marketing?

Checkpoint 1   PEARSON LONGMAN myacademicconnectionslab

3

Building Academic Reading Skills

In this section, you will learn about the organizational structure of written texts and how it relates to the purpose of the text.
For online assignments, go to

PEARSON LONGMAN
myacademicconnectionslab

Key Words

budget *n, v*
objective *n*
profit *n, v*
spend *v*
spender *n*
spending *n*
succeed *v*
successful *adj*
target audience *n*

Before You Read

1. *Draw a line from the word or expression on the left to its definition on the right. Then compare your answers with a partner's.*

budget *n, v* ———— pay money for something

objective *n* — the money a company makes; the difference between money coming in and money going out

profit *n, v* — producing the result you wanted; working in the way you wanted

spend *v* — the people who you want to see your advertising campaign; your goal is for these people to see your advertising

successful *adj* — something that you are working hard to complete

target audience *n* — a plan for money: how much to pay, and what to buy; the highest amount you will pay for something

2. *Complete the passage with the key words. Then compare answers with a partner's. You will not use all the words.*

Advertising is one of the most important things that most companies do to succeed. Without advertising, it would be difficult to make a (1) _____. No advertising means that no one knows about the company's products and services, so no one will buy them. Planning is very important. Companies must (2) _____ carefully. It is easy to (3) _____ too much money on advertising. They also must choose the right advertising (4) _____. If they get this wrong, the advertising might not be (5) _____, or the (6) _____ might not see the advertisements.

3. *The reading in the next section is an excerpt from a marketing textbook chapter. Read the overview of the chapter here. Then answer the question with a partner.*

In this chapter, you will learn about:

- Which different kinds of organizations advertise
- How to choose between four advertising goals

- How advertising budgets are decided
- How advertising strategies are chosen
- How advertising programs are evaluated

Companies advertise to sell their products. What other kinds of organizations might advertise? Explain.

Global Reading

Like lectures, written texts have an organizational structure. As with lectures, understanding and following the structure can help you understand the text.

For the explanation texts we're looking at in this unit, the stages are basically the same:

- The introduction includes a general statement and a scope, giving the main ideas.
- Each body paragraph shows the main ideas followed by the supporting ideas.
- The conclusion returns to the main ideas.

Just by reading one part of the introduction, you can quickly find your way to the main ideas.

1. *Complete the tasks. Then compare your answers with a partner's.*

1. Read paragraphs 1–3 of the textbook passage on pages 31–32. Answer the questions.

   a. In which paragraph is the scope? _____

   b. From the scope, what main ideas do you expect in the rest of the chapter?

   _____

2. Read all the headings. Answer the question.

   c. Which of the main ideas you listed for question **a** do you see in the headings?

   _____

   _____

3. Read paragraph 4. Answer the question.

   d. This paragraph has a mini-scope. From this, what main ideas will follow?

   _____

   _____

   _____

   _____

4. Read paragraphs 5-8. Answer the question.

   e. Did the reading cover all the points you listed in question **d**?

   _____

Knowing the **purpose** of a text helps us to understand it. Here are some common purposes:
- to give information
- to explain how and why people do something
- to show an opinion and the reasons for the opinion
- to advertise

You have probably noticed that there are a number of different types of organizational structure, such as process, opinion, and explanation. Each type of organizational structure has a different purpose. For example:
- process: to show the steps in a process
- opinion: to give reasons for an opinion
- explanation: to explain an idea

2. *Read the whole text. Then answer the questions.*

1. Which statement best describes the purpose of paragraphs 1–3?
   a. to show solutions to problems in advertising
   b. to show the steps in the process of planning an advertising campaign
   c. to explain the advantages and disadvantages of advertising

2. Which statement best describes the purpose of paragraphs 4–8, "Setting Advertising Objectives"?
   a. to explain different advertising objectives
   b. to show that one advertising objective is better than others
   c. to make you agree with the author

ADVERTISING

1   Advertising is very important. It can greatly help any organization to tell people about its goods and services. It is also very important for the economy. Advertisers in the United States now spend more than $264 billion a year. Around the world the figure is more than $550 billion. The world's largest advertiser is Proctor & Gamble. Last year, it spent almost $4 billion on U.S. advertising and more than $5.7 billion around the world.

2   Although advertising is used mostly by business, many other types of organizations also use it. These include not-for-profit organizations, professionals, and government agencies. They all advertise to various target audiences. In fact, the 25th largest advertising spender is a not-for-profit organization—the U.S. government. Advertising is a good way to inform and persuade, whether it is to sell Coca-Cola worldwide or to get people to take health precautions.

3   Marketers must make four important decisions when developing a successful advertising campaign. They must *choose advertising objectives, set the advertising budget, develop advertising strategy,* and *evaluate the advertising campaigns.*

(continued on next page)

Setting Advertising Objectives

4   The first step is to set an *advertising objective*. The objective is the purpose for the advertising campaign. There are four main advertising objectives—to *inform,* to *persuade,* to *compare,* or to *remind.*

5   Companies use *informative advertising* to give information about a new type of product. In this case, the purpose is to increase demand for the new product. DVD players are a good example. The first sellers of these products had to tell consumers about the quality and convenience of the new product. Big sales soon followed.

6   However, informative advertising doesn't work so well when there are many companies with the same kind of product. This is because consumers already know the normal features of the product. Instead, they need to see how one company's version is better than all the others. This kind of advertising is called *persuasive advertising.* For instance, when DVD players became common, Sony began trying to persuade customers that *its* brand has the best quality for their money to keep sales high.

7   *Comparative advertising* also tries to persuade. Thus it is really a kind of persuasive advertising. In this, a company compares its brand with one or more other brands. Comparative advertising has been used for products from soft drinks to car rentals and credit cards. An example is Avis, a car rental company, which compared itself with its bigger rival Hertz by claiming, "We're number two, so we try harder." This is a positive example, but comparisons in advertising can sometimes become quite negative. In some countries, this advertising strategy isn't used very much. In others, it is even banned.

8   A different kind of advertising is *reminder advertising*, which is important for products later in their life. Unlike the other types, its objective is to help to keep strong relationships with customers and to keep them thinking about the product. This is why expensive Coca-Cola television ads mainly build and maintain the Coca-Cola brand relationship, rather than trying to inform or persuade people to buy the drink straight away.

Setting the Advertising Budget

9   After deciding its advertising objectives, the company next *sets its advertising budget* for each product. No matter what method is used, setting the advertising budget is no easy task. Here, we look at four common methods used to set the total budget for advertising.

Source: Adapted from Armstrong, G., & Kotler, P. (2007). *Marketing: An introduction* (8th ed.). Upper Saddle River, NJ: Pearson Prentice Hall.

Focused Reading

1. Read the text again. Then answer the questions.

1. Which kinds of organizations are listed in the reading?

2. Complete the chart on the next page next by adding types of advertising next to their objectives. Then compare your answers with a partner's.

Type of Advertising	Objective
	To show that a product from one company is better than similar products from another company
	To show that a product has the best features
	To help people remember a product they already know about; to encourage people who already buy a product to keep on buying it
	To show people something new

Understanding Relationships within a Reading Text

The main reading in this unit is an explanation: it explains. Texts often explain by using these strategies:

- defining technical words
- giving examples
- giving a purpose or reason
- comparing (showing similarities) and contrasting (showing differences)

As with lectures, logical connectives show the relationships between ideas. From these, we can see which strategy is being used.

Example

Informative advertising works best for new products. However, if there are many similar products from other companies, persuasive advertising is better.

The logical connective *however* shows that the two sentences have opposite ideas. This is a contrast relationship. The example uses a contrast relationship to explain something about informative and persuasive advertising.

Texts with other purposes and structures (such as opinion texts and process texts) also use similar relationships.

2. Scan the text looking for the logical connectives in the box. Then put them in the correct column in the chart on page 34. Compare your answers with a partner's.

a different kind of . . .	but	rather than
because	however	to + verb

Purpose	Contrast	Reason
to + verb		

3. Work with a partner. Look at the structure of each paragraph in the reading on pages 31–32. Then look at the lists. Which paragraph is being described in each list? Write the paragraph number on the line. In many cases, the logical connectives will help you.

Paragraph: _____
- contrast (with previous advertising strategy)
- reason
- definition
- example

Paragraph: _____
- definition
- contrast
- reason

Paragraph: _____
- definition
- examples
- more information

Paragraph: _____
- purpose
- an example

4. Work with a partner. Imagine you are going to advertise the products listed. Answer the questions. Then share your ideas with the class.
- A car with a completely new kind of engine
- A popular and fashionable brand of clothing (not a new one)
- A new restaurant in an area popular for eating out

1. Which strategy from the reading would you use? Explain.

_____

_____

_____

_____

2. Would you use viral or stealth marketing? Explain.

_____

_____

_____

_____

Checkpoint 2 PEARSON LONGMAN myacademicconnectionslab

4

Building Academic Speaking Skills

In this section, you will practice expressing relationships between ideas. Then you will plan a marketing campaign, using either viral marketing or stealth marketing. You will use information from the reading and the lecture in this unit and from a radio talk you will hear to complete the task. For online assignments, go to

PEARSON LONGMAN
myacademicconnectionslab

Before You Speak

You will hear a professor giving students some advice about their assignment. The assignment is to plan a stealth or viral marketing campaign.

🎧 *Listen and take notes in the middle column. Then listen again and write the logical connectives you hear in the right-hand column. Compare your chart with a partner's.*

	What Does the Professor Say about the Message?	Logical Connectives
Point 1		
Point 2		
Strategy 1 (Point 2)		
Strategy 2 (Point 2)		

Focused Speaking

You are going to give a short talk of one to two minutes to practice using signals and logical connectives.

Expressing Relationships between Ideas

Just like the professors you hear, you should use signals and logical connectives in your talks. This will make the organizational structure, and the relationships between ideas, clear.

1. *Work with a partner. Choose one of the topics. Brainstorm ideas.*
  • three reasons to buy a product
  • three things a business can do to make people want to buy a product
  • three things a website can do to make people want to buy a product

2. Work alone to complete the outline about the topic you chose.

INTRODUCTION Ideas in the general statement: Main ideas in the scope:	
Main idea 1:	Details:
Main idea 2:	Details:
Main idea 3:	Details:
Conclusion:	

3. Compare your outline with a partner's. Which signals and logical connectives could you use in your talk? Tell your partner.

4. Find a new partner who chose a different topic. Take turns giving your short talk. Take notes as you listen. Check your understanding by showing your notes to the speaker.

Integrated Speaking Task

You have read a text and listened to a professor speak about marketing. You will now use your knowledge of the content, vocabulary, and academic skills presented in this unit to plan a campaign using stealth or viral marketing. You will also give a short talk explaining your campaign to other students.

Follow the steps to prepare your talk.

Step 1: Choose a product.

Work in two groups, A and B. Work with a partner from your group. Choose one product from your group's list.

Group A
- a snack food
- a film
- an airline

Group B
- an item of clothing
- a digital camera
- a hair salon

Step 2: Plan your talk.

Continue to work with your partner. Decide the features of your product and your campaign. Make notes in the chart. You will use them during your talk.

INTRODUCTION	
Ideas in the general statement: **Main ideas in the scope:**	
Main idea 1:	**Details: features**
Main idea 2:	**Details: why objective was chosen**
Main idea 3:	**Details: How will it work? What's the message? How will it spread?**
Conclusion:	

Step 3: Practice.
- Listen to your partner's talk. As you listen, take notes in the checklist on page 38.
- Change roles and repeat.
- Discuss your checklist with your partner. Suggest ways to make your talks better.

Step 4: Give the talk.
- Find someone from the other group.
- Listen to your new partner's talk. Use the checklist again.
- Change roles and repeat.
- Were the relationships between ideas clear in your partners' talks?

Presentation Checklist	Partner 1	Partner 2
Content What is the product?		
Did the campaign involve viral or stealth marketing?		
Are the advertising objectives appropriate?		
Structure Is there a clear preview/scope, showing main points?		
Are the relationships between ideas clear?		
Is there a clear conclusion?		

Step 5: Discuss.

After everyone has presented, discuss which marketing plans you think will be most effective.

UNIT
3

Astronomy
Collisions from Space

Unit Description

Content: This course is designed to familiarize the student with concepts in astronomy.

Skills: Coherence and Cohesion
- Recognizing reference in cohesion
- Recognizing logical connectives in lectures
- Listing ideas
- Writing cohesive texts

Unit Requirements

Readings: "What Killed the Dinosaurs?" (an excerpt from an astronomy textbook)

"Reports of a Major Collision" (a press release)

Lecture: "Are Asteroids and Comets Dangerous?"

Integrated Writing Task: Writing a paragraph about the usefulness of research into Near-Earth Objects (NEOs)

Assignments: www.MyAcademicConnectionsLab.com

1
Preview

For online assignments, go to

Previewing the Academic Content

Dinosaurs are perhaps the most well-known of extinct species. Children love them. Movies have been made about them. But where did they go? Their extinction is perhaps the biggest mystery in science. How did it happen? Has the same thing happened to other species? Whatever it was, could it happen again—to us? You will find out some answers to these questions in this unit.

1. Study the timeline. Then answer the questions in small groups.

Key Words

asteroid *n* a piece of rock in space, more than 33 feet (10 meters) across

collide *v* to crash into or hit another moving object; **collision** *n*

dinosaur *n* a type of reptile, mostly large, no longer living; lived in Mesozoic Era

extinct *adj* when all animals of a species are dead; **extinction** *n*

mass extinction *n* many species of an animal dying at the same time

species *n* a specific type of animal, plant, etc.

volcano *n* a mountain that sends out fire and hot rock from deep down in Earth

Major events in Earth's history

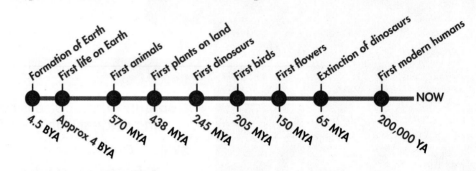

BYA: Billion (1,000,000,000) years ago
MYA: Million (1,000,000) years ago
YA: Years ago

1. For approximately what percentage of Earth's history have the following existed (90%, 50%, 10%, 1%, or <0.01%)?
   - animals _____
   - plants _____
   - life of any kind _____
   - modern humans _____

2. For how long did the dinosaurs live before they became extinct? How does this compare with how long humans have lived?

3. What surprises you the most about these dates?

4. What else do you know about dinosaurs?

5. What reasons have you heard to explain the extinction of dinosaurs?

2. *Read the excerpt from a scientific article. Answer the questions in small groups.*

1. Which was the biggest extinction event?
2. Which animals survived extinction events? Which animals did not?
3. Look at the gaps between these events. When might the next mass extinction happen?

THE "BIG FIVE" EXTINCTION EVENTS

It wasn't just the dinosaurs that died in mass extinctions: There have been many mass extinctions throughout history. In 1982, Jack Sepkoski and David Raup published an academic paper identifying the five largest extinction events in the history of the world. This research has been accepted by many scientists, and the events are now known as the "Big Five" mass extinction events. They are named for the period in history when they happened. For example, the "End Cretaceous Extinction" happened at the end of the Cretaceous period, the period when the dinosaurs were at their most powerful.

TIME	EVENT
444 million years ago	**End Ordovician Extinction Event** Many scientists believe this was the second largest mass extinction. Many species of early animals disappeared.
360 million years ago	**Late Devonian Extinction Event** This was a much slower event than the others. Over a period of 20 million years, about 70% of all species died.
251 million years ago	**End Permian Extinction Event** About 96% of all sea species and about 70% of land species, including plants and insects, died.
200 million years ago	**End Triassic Extinction Event** About 20% of all sea life and many species of land animals died out.
65 million years ago	**End Cretaceous Extinction Event** About 50% of all species, including the dinosaurs, became extinct.
TODAY	

Source: Raup, D.M., & Sepkoski, J. (1982). Mass extinctions in the marine fossil record. *Science, 215,* 1501–1503.

In this unit, you will learn about coherence and cohesion and how they can help you in reading, listening, and writing.

Previewing the Academic Skills Focus

Coherence and Cohesion

Coherence and **cohesion** are about how various parts of a text are connected. Understanding these will help you to follow texts and lectures. Using coherence and cohesion will help your writing and speaking seem natural and clear.

Read the paragraph. Then answer the questions with a partner.

There are many theories about the disappearance of the dinosaurs. The most accepted one at the moment is that Earth was hit by a large asteroid or comet. However, not all scientists agree with this. Some scientists think that the eruption of some very large volcanoes in India caused the extinction. Perhaps the answer is a combination of these factors.

1. What is the main idea of the paragraph? Are all of the sentences about that main idea? _____

   If so, the paragraph has **coherence**.

2. Look at the second sentence. What word earlier in the paragraph does the pronoun *one* refer to? _____

   This is an example of **referencing**—a type of cohesion. It uses words such as pronouns and demonstratives to refer to ideas mentioned earlier.

3. Look at the second and third sentences. What word shows a connection or relationship between these two sentences? _____

   What is the relationship between these two sentences? Circle one.

   cause/effect   *time*   *comparison*   *contrast*

   This is an example of a logical connective, another way to add cohesion.

Before You Read

Work with a partner. Look at the pictures, captions, and headings in the textbook excerpt on pages 43–44. Check (✓) the topics you think the text will include. Explain your answers. More than one answer is possible.

_____ History of life on Earth

_____ Explanations for mass extinctions throughout history

_____ Evidence that a meteorite collision killed the dinosaurs

_____ Danger from a catastrophe in the future

_____ The effect of climate on the dinosaurs

_____ Different opinions about the disappearance of the dinosaurs

2
Building Academic Reading Skills

In this section, you will practice recognizing cohesive devices in written texts.
For online assignments, go to

Global Reading

1. *Skim the text quickly. Number the ideas in the order they appear. Then compare your answers with a partner's.*

_____ There were ideas for their disappearance, but there was little evidence.

__1__ The dinosaurs' disappearance was mysterious and sudden.

_____ Could the same happen to us?

_____ A layer of iridium was discovered, which is evidence for the meteorite theory.

_____ The Chicxulub crater provided further evidence for the meteorite theory.

_____ No one knows how often these major catastrophes happen.

_____ A large meteorite can kill living things all around the world.

What Killed the Dinosaurs?

The Biggest Mystery in Earth's History

1 For many years, one of the biggest mysteries in science has been how the dinosaurs disappeared.

2 These amazing animals ruled Earth for 160 million years. They lived everywhere, on every continent. They were the largest and most powerful animals for a large part of the history of animal life on Earth. Compared with humans' two hundred thousand years or so, this is an amazing achievement. But, suddenly, about 65 million years ago, they all died. And it wasn't just the dinosaurs—interestingly, more than 50 percent of all animal species on Earth also disappeared. This is very surprising,

because there were very many different species of dinosaur, all suited to different climates and conditions. The normal causes of extinction, such as natural climate change, may explain why some species of dinosaur died out, but not all of them. As we will see, it seems likely that a major and sudden disaster caused their disappearance.

A Solution . . . Perhaps

3 So, what was this disaster? In the past, scientists thought of many possible explanations. These included disease, earthquakes, volcanoes, or even changes in the magnetic field of Earth. Unfortunately, for a long time, there was no strong evidence for any of them.

4 This changed, however, in 1980. Researchers, led by Nobel Prize winner Luis Alvarez, noticed something unusual. To help us explain what this

(continued on next page)

was, we have to know that rock is often in layers, each layer matching a different time in history.

Alvarez and his team were amazed to find that the layer of rock that matched the time of the dinosaurs' extinction 65 million years ago had a very large amount of something called iridium. And this wasn't just in one place—it was all around the world. Iridium is very unusual; there is very little of it on Earth. In fact, there was 30 to 130 times more of this material than normal in this layer of rock. What amazed the Alvarez team was that this was about the same amount as the percentage of iridium in meteorites.

meteorite crater in Arizona

5 How could this material spread all around Earth? Scientists can predict what might happen when a large asteroid hit Earth. The collision would send dust[1] up into the atmosphere. Winds would spread it around the world. It would stay in the atmosphere for several years, stopping sunlight. This would cause plants and trees to die. Because there would be less sunlight, the climate would also become dramatically cooler. Animals that used to eat the plants would starve,[2] as would the meat-eating animals that ate them. Dinosaurs, at the top of the food chain, would be the most vulnerable. No large animal can live for years without food.

Layers of rock in Lulworth, Dorset, England

More Evidence

6 By now, you might be thinking that there should be more physical[3] evidence, such as a crater where the asteroid hit. In 1990 scientists found just such a crater. The Chicxulub crater in Mexico is 112 miles (180 kilometers) across, just the size that the Alvarez team estimated. Scientists have worked out that the asteroid was probably about 6.2 miles (10 kilometers) across. The collision would have released 2 million times more energy than the largest nuclear bomb ever made.

Disagreement

7 So far, the evidence appears quite strong. However, not every scientist agrees. Some say that the iridium layer is thicker in some places than others. No one can find a full explanation for this. People who disagree with the meteorite theory say that volcanoes could have produced the same result.

8 Also, there is a small amount of evidence that not all dinosaurs died out. Archaeologists have found dinosaur fossils from up to a million years later than the mass extinction. However, other scientists question these claims.

Could It Happen Again?

9 To conclude, current evidence seems to point to a major catastrophe—most likely a meteorite. The big question now is: How often do similar events happen? This was not the only mass extinction in Earth's history—there were several others long before the dinosaurs. So, will humans be in danger from a similar event in the future?

---

[1] **dust** *n* very small particles of something, for example, sand or tiny pieces of rock
[2] **starve** *v* die because there isn't enough to eat
[3] **physical** *adj* something you can see or touch; not just an idea

Source: Adapted from Chaisson, E., & McMillan, S. (2005). *Astronomy today* (5th ed.). Upper Saddle River, NJ: Pearson Prentice Hall.

2. *Discuss the questions with a partner.*

    1. Are any of the main ideas on a different topic from the title?

    2. Based on your answer to question 1, does the text seem coherent? Explain.

Focused Reading

1. *Look at the first sentence of paragraph 2. Which word or words in the sentence before it does "These amazing animals" refer to?*

_____

Recognizing Reference in Cohesion

Writers in English use a lot of cohesive devices. They see this as good style. On page 42, you looked briefly at reference and transitions to build cohesion.

In particular, paying attention to reference can help you understand a text—it can help you keep track of the ideas.

These points can help you follow reference:

- Plurals refer to plurals, and singulars refer to singulars.
- Sometimes, reference can refer to a whole idea, not just a single word.

2. *Look at the underlined words in the sentences from the text. Circle the word or phrase they refer to. Connect them with an arrow. Then answer the questions that follow the example sentences.*

    1. One of the biggest mysteries of science for many years has been how the dinosaurs disappeared. These amazing animals ruled Earth for 160 million years. They lived everywhere . . .

    Which animals ruled Earth for 160 million years? _____

    2. They were the largest and most powerful animals for a large part of the history of animal life on Earth. Compared with humans' two hundred thousand years or so, this is an amazing achievement.

    What was the dinosaurs' amazing achievement? _____

    3. The layer of rock that matched the time of the dinosaur's extinction, 65 million years ago, had a very large amount of something called iridium. And this wasn't found just in one place—it was found all around the world.

    What was found all around the world? _____

(continued on next page)

4. Iridium is very unusual—there is very little of <u>it</u> on Earth. In fact, there was 30 to 130 times more of <u>this material</u> than normal in this layer of rock.

Why is iridium unusual? _____

How much more iridium was there than usual? _____

5. In fact, there was 30 to 130 times more of this material than normal in this layer of rock. What amazed the Alvarez team was that <u>this</u> was about the same as the percentage of iridium in meteorites.

How much more iridium is there in asteroids than is usual on Earth?

_____

3. *Read paragraph 5. Then work with a partner. Number the sentences in the correct order to explain how an asteroid collision could kill the dinosaurs.*

_____ These animals also die.

_____ Plant-eating animals don't have enough to eat.

_____ This causes temperatures to fall.

_____ The collision throws dust into the air.

_____ This forms a layer in the atmosphere, which cuts sunlight.

_____ This leads to their extinction.

_____ Trees and plants need sunlight.

_____ Winds spread it around Earth.

_____ When they can't get enough of it, they die.

_____ Because of this, meat-eating animals don't have enough to eat.

__*1*__ An asteroid collides with Earth.

4. *Work with a partner. Read the statements. Decide if they are true or false. Write* **T** *(true) or* **F** *(false). Then discuss the reasons for your answers.*

_____ 1. The Chicxulub crater was the right size to be the one caused by the asteroid that killed the dinosaurs.

_____ 2. The Chicxulub crater was easy to see.

_____ 3. All scientists in this field think the iridium layer was caused by volcanoes.

_____ 4. All scientists in this field think the dinosaurs died out at the same time as the iridium layer appeared.

_____ 5. Researchers need to find out how often meteorites collide with Earth.

_____ 6. Researchers need to find out whether some dinosaurs lived for a million years after the mass extinction.

5. *Work in small groups. Discuss the questions.*

1. After reading the text, what have you learned about what killed the dinosaurs?

2. Do you think Earth might be in danger? Why or why not?

3

Building Academic Listening Skills

In this section, you will practice listening for logical connectives and transitional devices in spoken English. This will help you to follow the main ideas in lectures. For online assignments, go to

myacademicconnectionslab

Before You Listen

Work in a small group. Look at the poster from the movie Deep Impact *and answer the questions.*

1. What do you think happens in the movie?

2. Do you think the events in the movie can really happen? Explain.

3. What would be the effect of this event for people? How might this happen?

4. How likely do you think this event is?

Global Listening

Recognizing Logical Connectives in Lectures

Professors often use questions or signals to show topic changes (main ideas) and conclusions. You saw some of these in Unit 1.

Signals, also called markers, in spoken English are sometimes the same as in writing (e.g., *However* and *To conclude*). But they are often more conversational (e.g., *OK, so, let's move on to the next topic* and *With that, I'll sum up today's lecture.*) Just as with written English, they often include logical connectives, showing the relationships between ideas.

It is a good idea to listen carefully in lectures for logical connectives and questions. They will help you follow the main ideas.

1. *Work with a partner. Write **S** next to markers that you think are used more in speaking. Write **W/S** next to those that are used both in writing or speaking. In the third column, write **introduction** if the marker marks an introduction; **topic change** if it marks a new topic or new main idea; and **conclusion** if it marks a conclusion.*

Marker	S or W/S?	What Does it Mark?
However,		
Now that we've talked about . . . , let's move on to . . .		
Let's look now at the most important step . . .		
Today we'll talk about . . .		
In conclusion,		
Next, we'll look at . . .		
The next question is . . .		
But . . .		

comet n an object in the sky like a very bright ball with a tail, that moves through space

destroy v to damage something so badly that it cannot be used or no longer exists; **destruction** n

explode v to burst into small pieces, making a loud noise and causing damage, or to make something do this; **explosion** n

2. ◠ *In the lecture, the professor asks the three questions. Listen to the lecture and write the professor's answers to her own questions. Take notes.*

1. You may have seen bad films such as *Deep Impact* or *Armageddon* . . . but is there any reality to them?

_____

_____

_____

2. The next important question is . . . what can . . . governments . . . do about it?

_____

_____

_____

3. But, if we find one heading straight toward Earth—the harder question is what to do then?

_____

_____

_____

3. *Does the professor think Earth is safe from a meteorite collision? Discuss in small groups.*

Focused Listening

1. ◠ *Listen to the lecture again. The professor gives two reasons why Earth does not have lots of craters. Write her reasons and the markers she uses to signal each reason.*

Reasons	Markers

In lectures, you will often hear lists of ideas, reasons, effects, etc. Lecturers will often use logical connectives to signal the lists, such as:

There are two . . .

The first is . . .

Also . . .

Noticing these expressions can help you know where each idea, reason, or effect starts and finishes.

Shooting stars

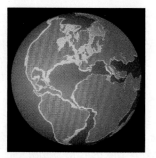

The world towards the end of the dinosaurs' time

2. 🎧 *Listen to the lecture again. Then answer the questions. Compare your answers with a partner's.*

1. How often do scientists think large asteroids hit Earth?

   _____

2. What happened in 1989?

   _____

3. How often do objects the same size as the 1989 one hit Earth?

   _____

4. Why wouldn't it work to destroy an asteroid heading for Earth?

   _____

5. What is the problem with changing an asteroid's direction?

   _____

3. *Work in small groups. Discuss your answer to the questions.*

1. Do you feel more or less in danger after hearing the lecture? Why?

2. Do you think governments should take this issue more seriously? Why or why not?

3. Look at the text on pages 43–44. When did scientists find the Chicxulub crater?

4. Why did it take so long to find the crater? Use ideas from the lecture in your answer.

Checkpoint 2   PEARSON LONGMAN **myacademicconnectionslab** 🚢

4

Building Academic Writing Skills

In this section, you will practice using techniques for cohesion. Then you will write a short essay about whether research into Near-Earth Objects (NEOs) is useful using information from the readings and the lecture in this unit.

For online assignments, go to

Before You Write

1. *Read the press release. Match the approximate size of the NEO with the damage it will cause and the chance it will happen in an average lifetime (80 years).*

Approximate size	Amount of damage	Chance it will happen in an average lifetime
13 feet (4 m) across	**worldwide catastrophe**	**unlikely**
300 feet (~100 m) across	**local damage**	**extremely unlikely**
.6 miles (~1 km) across or more	**no damage**	**quite likely**

CelesTek **FOR IMMEDIATE RELEASE: JANUARY 16**

REPORTS OF A MAJOR COLLISION

CelesTek Space Research Agency would like to clarify recent press reports that an asteroid is likely to hit Earth in 2018. Further measurements have now been taken, and we are now certain that this asteroid will not hit Earth.

We will continue with our efforts to find Near-Earth Objects (NEOs). We also aim to find out about the size, shape, composition, and structure of objects when we find them. This information will help the world to deal with dangerous asteroids if they are found.

With continued funding, we hope to have reached our goal of finding 90 percent of all objects that may collide with Earth by 2030.

To put the recent NEO into context, the following may be useful to know. Every year, an object the size of a car hits the atmosphere but burns up before reaching the surface. Every 1,000 years, an object the size of a football field hits Earth. This does cause significant damage in the local area, but the chances of it hitting a city are low. The last one was at Tunguska in Russia early last century. No one saw it; they only heard it. An object big enough to cause a serious catastrophe happens once every few million years.

While the threat is not great, it is likely that some time in the future history of humanity, research of the kind undertaken by CelesTek will enable serious disasters to be avoided.

For more information, contact the Public Information Officer at: http:// www.CelesTekSpaceResearch.org

2. *When you next hear on the news about an asteroid passing close to Earth, what will you think? Choose one of the opinions, or write your own. Share your opinion with the class.*

- "The news is making it sound more dangerous than it really is."

- "I wish the government would spend more money on NEO research."

- Your opinion: _____

Focused Writing

Writing Cohesive Texts

Cohesion is important in writing. Remember to use techniques for cohesion, including referencing and logical connectives in your writing.

1. *Read the text. Complete the sentences with the words from the box. Some words are not used, and some are used more than once.*

however	later	this
in addition	they	to conclude

Early one morning in June 1908, some of the few people near the forests of Tunguska, in north central Siberia, heard a strange noise. When they looked up, they saw a bright light, nearly as bright as the sun, moving quickly across the sky. A few minutes after (1) _____*this*_____, there was a bright flash and a very loud noise. (2) _____ was quickly followed by a shock wave that broke windows hundreds of miles away. For a few days after (3) _____ event, nights were so bright that people could read without lights. Fortunately, (4) _____ happened in a very remote area with very few people.

(5) _____, an expedition of scientists went to Tunguska to make maps. (6) _____ could easily see that a big disaster had happened, because for around 30 miles (50 kilometers), all the trees were flat on the ground. (7) _____ guessed that a meteorite had caused it. (8) _____, it was not until near the end of the twentieth century that this was confirmed. What most likely happened was that a large meteorite, about 200 feet (60 meters) across, got so hot that it exploded, about 5 miles (8 kilometers) above Earth.

2. *Write a paragraph to answer this question:* **Do you feel in danger from a collision with an asteroid? Explain.** *Follow the steps.*

Step 1: Think about the reasons for and against. Then decide whether you feel in danger from a collision.

Step 2: Choose a topic sentence that states your opinion.

Step 3: Write supporting details. These are the reasons for your opinion. While writing, pay attention to referring words and transitional devices.

Step 4: Check your paragraph. Pay attention especially to referring words and transitional devices. Make any changes as needed.

Integrated Writing Task

You have listened to and read about potential dangers of meteorites. You will now use your knowledge of the content and vocabulary from this unit to write a coherent and cohesive, four-paragraph essay in response to this question: **Some people say that NEO research can help protect Earth from a collision with an asteroid. Others say that it is a waste of money. Do you think that NEO research should continue?**

Follow the steps to write your essay.

Step 1: Think about the readings and lecture in this unit and decide on your answer to the question.

Step 2: Plan your paragraph by answering the appropriate questions in the chart for each section of your essay.

	If Your Answer to the Essay Question is *Yes,* Answer These Questions:	If Your Answer to the Essay Question is *No,* Answer These Questions:
Introduction	• What are NEOs? • Who is looking for them and why? • Is this good or bad?	• What are NEOs? • Who is looking for them and why? • Is this good or bad?
1st Body Paragraph	• What probably happened when an asteroid hit Earth in the past? • Could this happen again?	• What happened to the dinosaurs? • What probably caused it? • How long ago was this? • Has there been a similar extinction event since then? • How likely do you think it is that a similar asteroid will hit us?
2nd Body Paragraph	• What are scientists looking for now? • Are these projects cheap or expensive? • What problem might they prevent?	• What are scientists looking for now? • Do these projects cost a lot of money? How much? • What are other large problems that could kill people around the world? • Should money be spent on NEO research, or other life and death problems?

(continued on next page)

	If Your Answer to the Essay Question is *Yes*, Answer These Questions:	If Your Answer to the Essay Question is *No*, Answer These Questions:
Conclusion	• Do we have to be careful about asteroids? Why? • Is the research important? Why? • What might be the consequence of the research?	• Is an asteroid or comet likely to kill us? • Which problem has the largest effect now, NEOs or the ones you mentioned in the 2nd Body Paragraph? • Is NEO research wasting governments' money? Explain.

Step 3: Write your essay using your answers to the questions in the chart as a guide.

Step 4: Exchange your essay with another student. Comment on each other's essays. Use the checklist.

In the essay:	Yes
Is each paragraph about only one main idea?	
Does each body paragraph have a topic sentence? (See Unit 1.)	
Are the ideas linked with cohesive devices?	
Does the conclusion begin with a cohesive device for conclusions?	

Step 5: Based on your discussion with your partner, write a second draft of your essay and give it to your teacher.

UNIT 4

Acting
IMAGINATION

Unit Description

Content: This course is designed to familiarize the student with the role and use of the imagination in acting.

Skills: Summarizing

- Recognizing digressions and asides
- Distinguishing major from minor points
- Recognizing summary statements and conclusions
- Preparing spoken summaries

Unit Requirements

Lecture: "Using Your Imagination on Stage"

Readings: "Imagination: An Actor's Tool" (an excerpt from an acting textbook)

"Gladiator" and *"Elizabeth"* (movie synopses)

Integrated Speaking Task: Summarizing how an actor might use imagination when preparing for a role

Assignments:
www.MyAcademicConnectionsLab.com

1
Preview

For online assignments, go to

PEARSON LONGMAN
myacademicconnectionslab

Key Words

character *n* a person in a movie, play, or book

create *v* to make something new exist or happen

imagination *n* an ability to make a picture in your mind; **imaginary** *adj;* **imagine** *v*

play *n* a story performed by actors in a theater, with an audience watching

plot *n* the story in a movie, play, or book

realistic *adj* something that looks real

role *n* the character an actor plays

setting *n* the place and time in history of a film, play, or book

Previewing the Academic Content

People enjoy watching movies or going to the theater. It is a great way to relax and to escape to another world, the world of the film or the play. This works well if the movie or play is realistic and if the actors' performances are realistic. So, how can an actor make his or her performance as realistic as possible? In this unit you will find out why imagination is the key to successful acting.

1. *Work with a partner. Look at the pictures. Then answer the questions.*

1. What do the pictures tell you about the setting and characters? For example, is this in the past? Are the characters rich or poor? What else?

2. Which role do you think is most difficult to play? Why?

3. Which role would you most like to play? Why?

2. *When we say that someone is a "good actor," what do we mean? What skills does a good actor have? Discuss with the class.*

3. *Imagine you are going to play one of the roles in the pictures. What could you do to prepare for that role? Discuss in small groups.*
- watching films that have similar plots
- imagining something about the character

   What? _____
- other ideas:

   _____

   _____

   _____

In this unit, you will learn about the skills necessary for effective summarizing.

Previewing the Academic Skills Focus

1. *A synopsis is a summary of a film, book, or play. Read the synopsis of the movie* Wag the Dog. *Then answer the question.*

When a dog is happy, it wags its tail.

Wag the Dog

In real life, dogs wag their tails, and people choose their presidents. However, in this movie, the normal order of society is turned around. The U.S. president, played by actor Michael Belson, is involved in a scandal[1] just before the next election. Facing possible defeat, he consults a public relations (PR) expert,[2] played by Robert DeNiro. The PR expert suggests creating a false war, played by actors. He thinks a war will stop people from thinking about the scandal. With the help of a Hollywood director (Dustin Hoffman), he films a "war" in a secret location. The idea is that the president will become a peacemaker and end the war. Then the public will see him as a hero, forget the scandal, and vote for him. Thus, the president attempts to control the people, that is, the tail tries to wag the dog. At least, that is the plan. The reality turns out to be somewhat different.

---

[1] **scandal** *n* an event including shocking behavior

[2] **public relations expert** *n* someone who tries to help an organization look good, by controlling information about it

Which of these are true for the synopsis? Check (✓) all that apply.

❏ 1. It includes the main ideas in the plot.

❏ 2. It includes small supporting details about the plot.

❏ 3. It is much shorter than the movie it summarizes.

Summarizing

Summarizing means finding the most important information in a written or spoken text, leaving out less important details, and then using this information in writing or speaking.

You will often have to prepare summaries at university. Sometimes your assignment will be to present a summary in writing or in speaking. Other times, summaries will be part of a larger assignment, such as an essay.

When summarizing:

• Keep it short. Include the main ideas, not unimportant details.

• Write in your own words. Don't copy a lot of words from the original source.

2. *Work in small groups. Answer the questions.*

1. Is the synopsis of *Wag the Dog* a good summary? Explain.

2. Have you seen *Wag the Dog*?

If Yes
- Is the synopsis truthful?
- Which character could you imagine playing? Why?

If No
- After reading the synopsis, would you like to watch the movie? Why or why not?
- Can you imagine the situation happening in real life? In which country? Why?

Before You Listen

1. *Read the course notes. Then write the key words next to their definitions.*

> **LECTURE 4** Imagination
>
> **Guest speaker:** *Gene Blake*
>
> Mr. Blake has acted both in plays and in film, and has appeared in over 30 films. He has played a very wide range of roles, from different periods in history and sectors of society, and is well-known for giving very authentic performances. Now he teaches master classes at some of the most famous acting schools around the world. In today's lecture, Mr. Blake will explore the use of imagination, with examples from his own career, including his most challenging roles, such as playing a disabled person and a London gang member. His talk will include some of the processes that his use of imagination is based on. You will learn how imagination is actually used in the real life of a working actor.

1. _____ to be an actor in

2. _____ not able to use part of the body

3. _____ just like the real thing

4. _____ come from another source or idea

5. _____ social class, e.g., upper class, middle class

2. *Work with a partner. Answer the questions.*

1. Why do you think some college or university courses have guest lecturers?

2. What are three questions that you think Mr. Blake might answer when he speaks to the class? Write the questions in your notebook.

Global Listening

1. 🎧 *Listen to the lecture. Who speaks about these ideas? Write **P** (the professor), **G** (the guest speaker), or **X** (not mentioned). Then compare your answers with a partner's.*

_____ 1. Gene Blake's experience

_____ 2. a definition of the word *imagination*

_____ 3. why imagination is important

_____ 4. how to start preparing for a new role

_____ 5. example of a disabled character

_____ 6. celebration and partying

_____ 7. a character from a book

_____ 8. using personal experience

Recognizing Digressions and Asides

Sometimes lecturers go off their main point (**digressions**) or tell stories that are related to the point but not an important part of it (**asides**). They do this to make the talk interesting.

It is important to recognize when the lecturer is digressing or giving an aside, and when the lecturer is making a major point. Digressions and asides often sound like small stories rather than statements of fact.

Do not include digressions or asides in summaries.

2. *Work with a partner. Which point from Exercise 1 is a digression or an aside?*

3. *Work with a partner. What is the lecture mainly about? Write two or three sentences in your notebook to summarize the lecture.*

Focused Listening

1. 🎧 *The following statements are false. Read them and then listen to the first part of the lecture. Change each statement to make it true. Then compare your answers with a partner's.*

1. Gene Blake now teaches master classes at theaters around the world.

_____

2. Imagination is any process in which we talk about anything that we are not currently experiencing.

_____

3. Imagination can be based on personal experience only.

_____

It is important to notice the difference between major and minor ideas when listening to a lecture. Remember that a summary contains only the major points. To find the major points, ask:

- Is the idea the speaker's main point?
- Is the idea a reason or an explanation of the main point?
- Is the idea signaled with expressions such as *Most importantly* or *First of all*?

If you cannot answer *yes* to any of these questions, the point is probably minor. Examples, digressions, and asides are often minor points, so they are usually not useful for summaries.

2. Which of the ideas you corrected in Exercise 1 is a minor point? Explain.

3. ⌒ Work in two groups: A and B. Look at the statements for your group only. Then listen to the second part of the lecture, and complete the statements.

Group A

1. Imagination can help an actor play a role _____.

2. An actor should understand the character's _____.

3. An actor playing a historical role must understand _____.

4. Researching a role includes reading and spending time with

   _____.

5. Gene spent a lot of time with _____ while preparing for his role.

6. Someone became _____ with Gene.

7. _____ experiences shape adults' thoughts and feelings.

Group B

1. Actors need imagination because their character's life might be _____ from their own.

2. Gene's first step with a new role is to _____.

3. Gene's disabled character couldn't move _____.

4. Gene imagined he was _____ while preparing for his role.

5. Gene thought a lot about his character's _____.

6. Gene once played a gang member from _____.

7. Gene used his experiences in _____ to help him understand the gangs in London.

4. Work with someone from the other group. Share your answers to Excercise 3. Then look at all the statements together. Discuss which points are major and which are minor. Mark the major points **MJ**, and the minor points **MN**.

5. Work in small groups. Discuss the questions.

1. Think back to your answers in Exercise 3 on page 56. After hearing the lecture, how would you prepare differently for the roles you talked about in that exercise?

2. Next time you watch a film, how will you think differently about the acting?

3. In what ways has the lecture helped you understand acting better?

Checkpoint 1   PEARSON LONGMAN myacademicconnectionslab

3
Building Academic Reading Skills

In this section, you will practice recognizing summary statements and conclusions in written texts.

For online assignments, go to

PEARSON LONGMAN
myacademicconnectionslab

Before You Read

Work with a partner. Match the statements about acting on the left with their reasons or explanations on the right.

_____ 1. Actors have to think about many aspects of their characters' lives and experiences.

_____ 2. Early humans needed imagination to survive.

_____ 3. Actors and artists have to use creativity.

_____ 4. Actors use many tools.

a. By imagining dangers, they could avoid them.

b. These include their skills in using their body, voice, imagination, feelings, and action.

c. If they just used old ideas, people would be less interested in watching them.

d. By doing this, they can really understand their roles.

Global Reading

Recognizing Summary Statements and Conclusions

Many texts summarize their main ideas in the introduction. As you saw in Unit 2, this part of the introduction is called the scope. They may also have a summary at the end in the conclusion.

Texts that follow this kind of pattern include: chapters of a textbook, sections within chapters, and essays.

When skimming, noticing the summary statements in the introduction and conclusion can help you find the main ideas quickly.

1. *Read the first and last paragraphs of "Imagination: An Actor's Tool." Underline the statements that summarize the main ideas of the text. Then discuss any differences with a partner.*

IMAGINATION:
AN ACTOR'S TOOL

(from *Acting: An Introduction to the Art and Craft of Playing* by Paul Kassel)

1　The imagination is at the center of creativity and is the most powerful of the actor's tools. In this section, we will see where imagination came from and, most importantly, we will look at how and why we can use imagination to help our acting. We will see that effective use of imagination will help us keep the attention of the audience and make our performances authentic and believable.

2　No one knows where imagination came from. But it is clear that early humans could feel in their mind a vision, a sound, a smell, a touch, an emotion that was not related to their present—if they used imagination. It may have been, originally, a way to survive. For example, humans could not easily smell a dangerous bear in a cave. But when looking at a dark cave, they may have remembered past experiences of bears. And they may have seen a bear coming out of a cave in the past. From these experiences, they could imagine that there *might* be a bear inside. Thus, they could avoid the danger. Modern humans are no different. Our normal lives present us every day with dark caves and, by imagining what might happen, we decide what to do.

3　The process of acting is no different. Just as with other human tasks, artists choose and use whatever ideas are most useful for their art. In a way, each play presents a dark cave, really a whole world for artists to imagine. Artists need to imagine how their characters might behave, how their characters are feeling, and how past events in their characters' lives have affected them. By doing this, they can make their characters seem more real.

4　The audience is also important—we, as actors, need to help our audiences to use their imaginations. The more authentic and truthful your performance, the more believable you appear, and the more you pull your audience into the world of the play or film.

5   Much of this authenticity is in your preparation for the role. It is important as an actor to think about the character's likely feelings and actions in each situation. Psychologists tell us that many of people's reactions come from their life experiences. We have to think through two things. We have to consider not only how the character develops during the play, but also the character's life experiences. These might have affected the character's lifetime development.

6   It is not surprising, then, that using the imagination is an important part of Stanislavsky's "system." Stanislavsky summarized this point by saying "*if* is the most useful word in an actor's vocabulary." He called this word the "magic if." He believed that "if" is the key that opens up the door to the imagination. We think about the situation we have to act out, and ask ourselves "what if" about every aspect of the situation. In this way, we can explore different possibilities. From this, we can decide which appears the most truthful, believable, and authentic.

7   Let's look at an example. Imagine your character is a knife murderer. For most people, this is very far from their own life experience! Why would someone kill other people? We have to use the imagination to find out. We explore possibilities. Perhaps your father was a drunk and treated your mother badly. Or it might be that you were seriously hurt at a young age by someone you trusted. Or you might have been bullied[1] at school, and had no friends or close family to turn to. Would that make you hate society, or hate certain kinds of people?

8   By going through this process, we can imagine the mind of our character, their feelings, and their reactions in the situation in which we have to portray them. A play or a film only has a couple of hours or so of storytelling time, but we have to portray a lifetime of experience. We have to imagine far more about the character than the play or the film script alone tells us.

9   So, now we can see where imagination comes from, how it helps our acting and why we have to work hard to let it work well. It is up to you now to apply this to your own performances, to make them appear as authentic to the audience as you can.

---

[1] **bullied** *v* threatened or hurt by someone bigger or stronger

Source: Adapted from Kassel, P. (2007). *Acting: An introducton to the art and craft of playing.* Boston: Pearson Allyn & Bacon.

2. Read the whole text quickly. Then summarize the important points in the text by completing the statements with words from the box.

audience	imagination	preparation	survive
early humans	imagining	similar	

1. Imagination may have developed as a way to help early humans to

   _____.

2. Using imagination in acting is _____ to how

   _____ used imagination.

3. Actors need to help their _____ to use their imagination.

4. To make a performance appear authentic to the audience,

   _____ is important. Imagination is part of this.

5. _____ is important in Stanislavsky's "system".

6. _____ a character's feelings and reactions can help actors

   show more about the character than the script tells us.

3. Are there any main ideas that were not covered by the summary statements you underlined in Exercise 1?

4. Which point from Exercise 2 would you most like to find out more about? Explain.

Focused Reading

1. Review the ideas in Before You Read on page 61. Then scan the text on pages 62–63 and decide which of these ideas are stated in the text. If an idea is stated, write the paragraph number on the line.

_____ 1. Actors have to think about many aspects of their characters' lives and experiences.

_____ 2. Early humans needed imagination to survive.

_____ 3. Actors and artists have to use creativity.

_____ 4. Actors use many tools.

2. *Read the text again and take notes in the outline on supporting details.*

Main Idea 1: *Imagination may have developed as a way to help early humans to survive.*

    Supporting Details:

Main Idea 2: *Using imagination in acting is similar to how early humans used imagination.*

    Supporting Details:

Main Idea 3: *Actors need to help their audience to use their imagination.*

    Supporting Details:

Main Idea 4: *To make a performance appear authentic to the audience, preparation is important. Imagination is part of this.*

    Supporting Details:

Main Idea 5: *Imagination is important in Stanislavsky's "system."*

    Supporting Details:

Main Idea 6: *Imagining a character's feelings and reactions can help us show more about the character than the script tells us.*

    Supporting Details:

3. 🎧 *Look at the chart. It gives information on two topics from the reading. Listen to the lecture again, and complete the chart with details you hear. Then compare your chart with a partner's.*

Topics	Point from the Reading	Related Point from the Lecture
Preparing for Roles	Actors need to prepare for their roles by thinking about the character's feelings and actions.	
Using Imagination	Actors need to imagine their character's behavior.	

Checkpoint 2

4

Building Academic Speaking Skills

In this section, you will prepare a spoken summary. You will imagine that you are an acting student and summarize how you would prepare to play a role in a movie. For online assignments, go to

Before You Speak

1. *As a class, divide into two groups: A and B. Read your group's movie synopsis.*

Group A

Synopsis of *Elizabeth*

1   It's England year 1558. Queen Mary, a Catholic, has just died. Her younger Protestant sister, Elizabeth, becomes the next queen. But there are many problems and difficulties. Bad feelings between Catholics and Protestants are so strong that many Protestants have been executed[1] because of their religion.

---
[1] **executed** *v* killed as a punishment

2   Elizabeth finds herself surrounded by people wanting to advise her. But they all want to influence her, mostly through marriage. Her companion through her early years is her childhood sweetheart, Robert Dudley, Earl of Leicester. Dudley is from a rich family, and has been in prison for earlier problems with the royal family. He is a handsome man and popular with the ladies. They were very close before Elizabeth became queen. But can she still trust him? And what about all the other "advisors"?

3   At the beginning of the film, we see Elizabeth as a young person, not experienced in dealing with people she does not trust. As time goes by, her experience grows and so does her ability to make difficult decisions. To survive, she must order executions. But what about her relationship with Dudley? She knows that if she marries, she will give up some of her power . . .

Group B

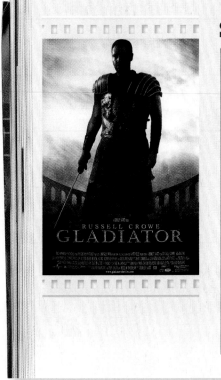

Synopsis of *Gladiator*

1   Maximus is a well-known leader in the army of Rome, the strongest power in Europe 2,000 years ago. He has recently returned from a big victory. He is widely respected as a good person. In contrast, Commodus is the cruel, power-hungry son of the Roman Emperor. Maximus has been promised by Commodus's father, Marcus Aurelius, that he will be given great power over the Empire. However, Commodus has other ideas.

2   When Commodus hears of his father's plans, in a fit of anger he immediately murders his father and sends soldiers to murder Maximus and his family. Maximus escapes, but his family does not. Slave[1] traders capture him and he becomes a gladiator—a slave who fights to the death for people's entertainment.

3   Maximus is very successful as a gladiator and becomes famous for being brave, strong, and skillful. He survives some very dangerous situations. Eventually, he fights against the evil Commodus himself. Who will win?

---

[1] **slave** *n* a person who has no freedom and is forced to work for others

2. Complete the chart for the synopsis you read. Then compare your answers with a partner's in your group.

Name of film	
Setting	
Period in history	
Names of main character(s)	
Sector of society	

3. Work with a partner from the opposite group. Take turns telling each other about the synopsis you read. Fill in the chart for your partner's synopsis.

Name of film	
Setting	
Period in history	
Names of main character(s)	
Sector of society	

4. Work as a class. What life experiences may have influenced the two main characters' personalities? Explain. Use information from the synopses, and speculate as much as you like.

Focused Speaking

1. *Look at the steps for preparing spoken summaries in the box. How useful do you think each step is? Discuss your ideas with a partner.*

Preparing Spoken Summaries

Here is a suggested process for preparing spoken summaries:

Step 1: Note the main ideas of the text(s) you are summarizing.
Step 2: Make notes of your main ideas without looking at your source texts.
Step 3: Check your notes against the source texts. Change them if necessary.
Step 4: Practice your spoken summary with a partner.
Step 5: Discuss how to improve your summary. Change your notes if necessary.
Step 6: Practice again by yourself or with a partner.

Speaking from notes is better than writing every word, because preparation is quicker and you will sound more natural when speaking.

2a. *Prepare an oral summary to answer this question:* **How can actors use imagination to improve their performance?** *Follow the steps in the skills box above. Note that you have already completed part of Step 1 in the outline on page 65. Add notes if you like.*

2b. *Work with a partner. Listen to each other's summaries. While listening, complete the checklist.*

Does the summary include. . .	Yes
all major points?	
only important details?	
the speaker's own words?	

3. *Continue working with your partner. Give each other feedback. Use the checklist to help you answer the questions.*
- Whose summary was shorter?
- Were any important ideas missing?
- How can you improve your presentation?

4. *Using a similar process, prepare a summary of the movie synopsis you read.*

Integrated Speaking Task

You have read a text and listened to a lecture about the use of imagination in acting. You have also read synopses of two movies. You will now use the content, vocabulary, and summarizing skills from this unit to give a short talk in answer to this question: **How is imagination useful to an actor preparing for a role? Illustrate your answer with reference to a particular role.**

Follow the steps to prepare your talk.

Step 1: Work with a partner. Think of a film you both know well or think again about the film in the synopsis you read. Then each of you should choose a different character to discuss from that film.

Step 2: Together, discuss and decide how you will each prepare for the role. Use some of the ideas from the lecture and the reading in this unit.

Step 3: Prepare your talk. You can use your notes from the exercises in Before You Speak on page 68. Use the chart to organize your ideas. Remember to think about organizational structure (See Unit 2).

	Your Notes
Actors use their imagination to . . .	
Our film was about . . .	
The characters were . . .	
To prepare for the role ourselves, we discussed . . .	
In the end, we decided to . . .	
To conclude . . .	

Step 4: Practice your talk with your partner. Complete the Practice column of the checklist in Step 5. Suggest ways to improve.

Step 5: Find another partner who chose a different film. Give your talks to each other. While listening, complete the Final column in the checklist. Then give each other feedback.

Content Is there a clear, short summary . . .	Practice	Final
about imagination?		
of the movie and the character?		
of ideas for using imagination with the character?		
Features of a Summary Does the summary include . . .	Practice	Final
all the major points?		
no unimportant details?		
the speaker's own words?		

UNIT 5

Psychology
Emotions

Unit Description

Content: This course is designed to familiarize the student with concepts in psychology.

Skills: Synthesizing Information

- Recognizing abstract ideas and concrete examples
- Recognizing relationships between ideas from two spoken sources
- Writing summary statements in paragraphs
- Synthesizing information in writing

Unit Requirements

Readings: "What Do Our Emotions Do for Us?" (an excerpt from a psychology textbook)

"Emotions" (sample paragraphs)

Lecture: "Culture in Emotions"

Integrated Writing Task: Writing a paragraph about where emotional responses come from

Assignments: www.MyAcademicConnectionsLab.com

Previewing the Academic Content

We all experience emotions, and we all want to know how other people feel. But how do people communicate their emotions? And from the different ways to communicate emotions, which come from instinct, and which do we learn from the people around us? In this unit, you will find out answers to these questions—and more.

1. *Think about a time when you experienced a positive emotion. Work in small groups to answer the questions.*

1. What emotion did you experience?

2. What was the situation?

3. What did you feel like doing?

4. What did you do next? Why?

Key Words

contempt *n* a feeling that someone or something doesn't deserve any respect; **contemptuous** *adj*

disgust *n* a very strong, negative feeling about something shocking or unpleasant, such as food that tastes bad

frown *n, v* the expression on a person's face when they are worried, unhappy, or angry

instinct *n* something natural for you, not something you learned; **instinctive** *adj*; **instinctively** *adv*

recognize *v* to notice what something is because you have seen it or heard it before; **recognition** *n*

2. *Work in small groups. Complete the chart. First, try to use the key words or words from your own knowledge. Use a dictionary if you have to. Then tell your group about times when you experienced some of these emotions.*

Emotion		Facial Expression
Adjective	**Noun**	**(words may be used more than once)**
	happiness	
angry		
disgusted (by)		
sad		
surprised (by)		
	fear	
contemptuous (of)		

3. Look at the pictures. Match them with the first seven emotions in the chart on page 74. Compare your answers with a partner's. Discuss any differences in your answers.

4. Read the paragraph. Does the information surprise you? Explain.

> Psychologists have looked carefully at emotions and facial expressions. They have found that for some emotions, people from all cultures recognize the facial expression. These emotions are happiness, anger, disgust, sadness, surprise, fear, and possibly contempt. However, other emotions are not always recognized by other cultures.

In this unit, you will practice synthesizing information. You will also learn to recognize and use abstract ideas and concrete examples.

Previewing the Academic Skills Focus

Synthesizing Information

Synthesizing means combining information or ideas from different sources. For example, the sources could be a lecture and a textbook, or two different textbooks.

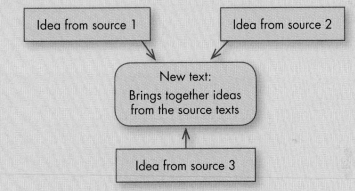

When you synthesize information, it is best to use your own words.

In an academic setting, you will have to synthesize information when you write essays, take part in class discussions, and prepare talks.

1. Read the paragraph from a psychology textbook. Then underline the main idea.

> Many psychologists have studied emotions. They want to know why humans have emotions, and also, how emotions can help us. This is an important subject, because emotions can very strongly affect our behavior.

alert *adj* being very focused on everything nearby

behavior *n* a person's typical actions or way of being; **behave** *v*

concentrate *v* to think very hard about something; **concentration** *n*

conscious *adj* aware that something is happening

flight *n* the act of running away or escaping

heart *n* the part of the body that causes blood to move around the body

senses *n* the ways that the body gets information from outside (e.g. through the eyes, ears, or nose)

sensitive *adj* able to notice small changes

2. 🎧 *Listen to an excerpt from a lecture on the same topic as the paragraph in Exercise 1. As you listen, take notes. Then, write one or two sentences to summarize what you heard.*

_____

_____

3. *Imagine that your professor asks this question:* **Why is the study of psychology important? Give an example to illustrate your answer.** *Check (✓) the answer that gives the best synthesis of the information from what you just read and listened to.*

❏ When people become frightened, their hearts beat faster. They become more alert, they concentrate harder and they become more aware of their surroundings. Their senses become more alert.

❏ Studying emotions is important because emotions have a big effect on our behavior. For example, when people are frightened, their body becomes more alert and their senses become more sensitive. They become more ready for fight or flight.

❏ Many psychologists have studied emotions. They want to know why humans have emotions, and also, how emotions can help us. This is an important subject because emotions can very strongly affect our behavior. One emotion that psychologists have studied a lot is fear. When someone is frightened, their body gets ready for fight or flight.

4. *Work with a partner. Use the diagram to explain your answer to the question in Exercise 3. Complete the diagram and discuss your answers.*

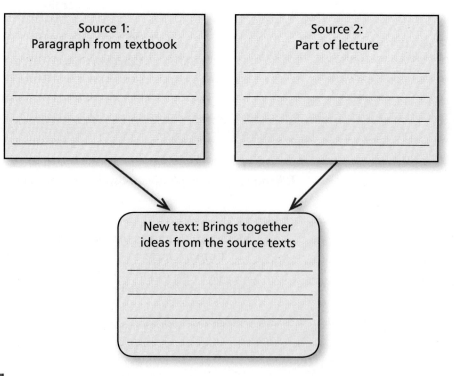

Source 1:
Paragraph from textbook

_____

_____

_____

Source 2:
Part of lecture

_____

_____

_____

New text: Brings together
ideas from the source texts

_____

_____

_____

_____

2

Building Academic Reading Skills

In this section, you will practice differentiating between abstract ideas and concrete examples. For online assignments, go to

PEARSON LONGMAN
myacademicconnectionslab

Before You Read

1. *Think about a stressful event that you have experienced, such as an exam or being late for an appointment. Then tell a partner.*

1. What was the event?

2. How did you feel physically and emotionally?

3. How did you want to respond at that moment?

2. *Work with a partner. First, read the list of physical responses that happen when a person experiences strong emotions such as fear. Then look at Figure 5.1. Label the places in the body with the physical responses from the list.*

Physical Responses

- Sweating increases
- Heart beats faster and stronger
- Brain becomes more alert
- Lungs get ready to take in more air
- Breathing becomes faster
- Skin becomes whiter because the blood vessels become narrower
- Sight becomes more sensitive
- Hearing becomes more sensitive

1. _____
2. _____
3. _____
4. _____
5. _____
6. _____
7. _____
8. _____

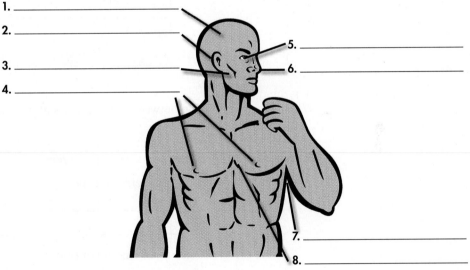

Figure 5.1 Physical response in humans to danger

3. *Tell your partner more about the event you mentioned in Exercise 1 or another stressful event.*

1. Which of the physical responses did you experience?

2. What physical responses do you generally experience in stressful situations?

3. What can you do to control these responses?

4. Why do you think humans have emotions? Explain.

Global Reading

1. *The diagram represents the main ideas of the reading in this unit and how the ideas relate to one another. Skim the reading on pages 79–80 quickly, and write the main ideas from the list in the diagram.*

Main Ideas

- The stages in an emotional response
- General ideas about emotions
- Question 1 to be answered in the body of the text
- Question 2 to be answered in the body of the text
- The reason that emotions exist, and how they develop

What Do Our Emotions Do for Us?

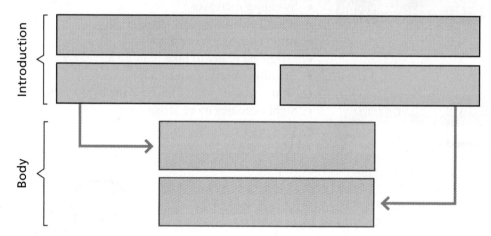

What is the relationship between the questions at the end of the introduction and the body of the text?

2. *Skim and scan the text to answer the questions.*

1. What are two things that emotions involve?

   _____

   _____

2. What are the stages in an emotional response?

   _____

   _____

3. Why did emotions develop?

   _____

   _____

WHAT DO OUR EMOTIONS DO FOR US?

Key Words

arousal *n* a physical-emotional state in which a person is alert and his or her heart is beating fast

gesture *n* a movement of hands or head, which communicates something

interpretation *n* the way people understand something (sometimes people may interpret the same thing in different ways); **interpret** *v*

jealousy *n* feeling angry or unhappy because someone has something you want; **jealous** *adj*

temperament *n* how people respond emotionally, in general

1   Winning an award, the death of a parent, an insult, losing a lover to someone else: All cause strong feelings—excitement, sadness, anger, jealousy. But what do these have in common? That is, why do we call them all "emotions"? The common theme is this: All emotions involve physical responses as well as responses in the mind.

2   And what purposes do these emotional responses have? Surely emotions must do more than just add variety or "color" to our lives. The brief answer to the question is that emotions help us respond to important situations and communicate our thoughts to others.

3   In this section, we will first consider what happens in our bodies when we experience emotions. Then we will look at how and why emotions developed.

What happens when we experience emotions?

4   In brief, emotional responses have four parts. There is a bodily (physiological) response, an interpretation in the mind, feelings, and an effect on behavior. These do not happen in any special order—they happen at the same time and affect each other. We will illustrate this process with the most carefully studied of all emotions: Fear.

5   To understand the physiological response, imagine you are frightened by an aggressive, noisy dog. Your brain sends messages throughout your body. It does this by releasing a chemical called adrenaline, which the blood carries to other parts of the body. Then, the bodily sensations of being frightened begin. Blood drains from your stomach (giving a feeling we describe as a "knot in the stomach"). The blood vessels in the face become narrower (which makes you become whiter). Similar processes exist for other emotions. With anger, for example, more blood flows to the hands, and more energy is released. This helps the person get ready for a fight.

6   The second aspect of emotion is interpretation in the mind of events and feelings. This is both conscious and unconscious. In fact, the more you think about the dog, the more frightened you become. Thinking like this sends both your feelings and your physical arousal to new heights.

7   The "feeling" aspect of emotions comes from two sources. In one, the brain senses the body's state of arousal. The other comes from memories of your body's reactions in similar situations in the past. So, when you see the angry dog, your brain may remember your feelings from past experiences with angry dogs.

8   Finally, emotions can also affect behavior. In response to the aggressive dog, this could be the so-called "fight-or-flight" response which appears to be part of our biology. In this, the person either becomes aggressive or runs away. Responses may also include facial expressions and sounds, such as crying, screaming or shouting. There may also be gestures, such as waving arms.

(continued on next page)

How and why did emotions develop?

9   Whether they happen in humans, cows, cats, or kangaroos, emotions are useful for survival. Fear, for example, undoubtedly helped people thousands of years ago to respond to dangerous situations—so that they became our ancestors,[1] not meals for dangerous animals. Similarly, the emotion we call love may attach us to a family; this helps us to continue our family line. This theory suggests that some emotional responses are built in to us—that is, they are biological.

10   We should make clear, however, that emotions are not completely fixed by our biology. They also involve learning, including learning from experience. Experiences from early in life are especially important because they set our emotional temperament. Experiences that involved strong emotional responses are also important. This is why a bad experience as a young child can have an effect much later in life. For example, if a dog attacks someone, that person may stay afraid of dogs for many years.

---

[1] **ancestors** *n* people in your family who lived a long time ago

Source: Adapted from Zimbardo, P., Johnson, R. L., Weber, A. L., & Gruber, C. W. (2007). *Psychology, AP Edition*. Upper Saddle River, NJ: Pearson Prentice Hall.

Focused Reading

Recognizing Abstract Ideas and Concrete Examples

You can sometimes help to make ideas clearer by synthesizing. For example, you might look for concrete examples from one source to illustrate abstract ideas in another source. One source does not have to be written or spoken: It can be from your own experiences.

Concrete examples are about things you <u>can</u> see or touch, such as actions, people, or machines.

Abstract ideas are about things you <u>cannot</u> see or touch, such as feelings and relationships.

1. *Work with a partner. Look at the first paragraph of the reading. It lists four emotions and concrete examples of what causes these emotions. Complete the chart.*

Abstract Idea (Emotion)	Concrete Example of a Cause of the Emotion
excitement	
sadness	
anger	
jealousy	

2. Work with a partner. Scan the reading for examples of what happens when we experience strong emotions such as fear. Write the examples in the middle column in the chart, including the paragraph number. Then complete the right-hand column with examples from Figure 5.1 on page 77 and your partner's life.

Idea	Examples from the Reading	Examples from:
Physiological response		Figure 5.1
Interpretation in the mind		
Feelings coming from memory		your partner's life
Emotions having an effect on behavior		your partner's life

3. Work with a partner. Would the author of the text agree or disagree with the statements? Circle the correct answer. Give evidence from the reading.

1. Emotions help cats to survive.
   a. agree   b. disagree

2. Fear helped early humans to survive.
   a. agree   b. disagree

3. Emotions come only from our biology.
   a. agree   b. disagree

4. Very frightening experiences at any stage in life may affect how you feel about similar experiences later in life.
   a. agree   b. disagree

4. *Discuss the questions with a partner.*

1. What new ideas did you learn from the reading?

2. Which of these was most interesting to you? Why?

3. Where else might you read about the ideas from the text outside a psychology class?

Checkpoint 1 ᴾᴱᴬᴿˢᴼᴺ ᴸᴼᴺᴳᴹᴬᴺ myacademicconnectionslab

3
Building Academic Listening Skills

In this section, you will practice recognizing relationships between ideas from different speakers.
For online assignments, go to

Before You Listen

Work in groups of three. Discuss the questions listed in the first column in the chart. Take notes on your discussion. After you discuss the questions, complete the chart.

Questions	Notes		
	Your Answers	Partner 1	Partner 2
1. What are some ways other than talking to communicate emotions?			
2. Are these ways instinctive or learned?			
3. Which of these ways to communicate emotions are the clearest?			
4. Which of these ways to communicate can people from other cultures recognize?			

Global Listening

1. 🎧 *Listen to the lecture and take notes about the main ideas in the chart.*

Key Words	Question	Notes about Your Answers
body language *n* communication through body position and body movements	1. What are some ways other than talking to communicate emotions?	
posture *n* body position when sitting or standing	2. Are these ways instinctive or learned?	
remote *adj* far away from where people live	3. Which of these ways to communicate emotions are important?	
	4. Which of these ways to communicate can people from other cultures recognize?	

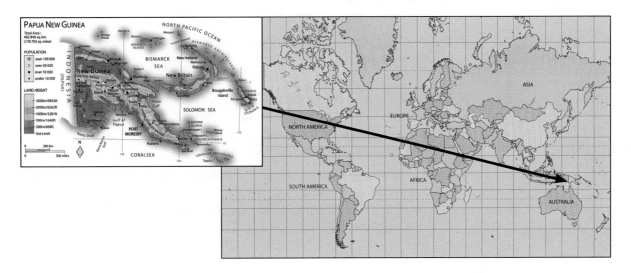

As stated earlier, synthesizing information from different sources can help you to answer questions from your professor and to complete assignments. It helps to notice the relationship between the different ideas in these sources.

Here is one process you can use to synthesize spoken ideas:

- Take notes about what each person said.
- Choose the ideas in your notes that relate to your task.
- Prepare your answer. Include the logical connectives that show relationships between these ideas.

As you learned in Units 1 and 2, relationships between ideas can include:

- Idea / example
- Idea / definition
- Steps in a process
- Opinion / reasons
- Idea / explanation

2. Work with a partner. Take turns giving a short talk to each other. Answer the questions. Use the information from the lecture and from your earlier discussions with other students.

How was what you heard in the lecture similar to what you discussed with your partner? How was it different?

Focused Listening

1. 🎧 Read the statements. Then listen to the lecture again. As you listen, circle the correct answer to complete each statement. Then discuss your answers with a partner.

1. _____ suggest strong emotions.
   a. Smiles and frowns
   b. Frequent, fast movements

2. Postures fall into the category of body _____.
   a. language
   b. movement

3. Meeren and other researchers found that people use _____ to see others' emotions.
   a. body language more than facial expression
   b. facial expressions more than body language

4. Many psychologists think that emotional expression helped people to enjoy _____. This helped them to _____.
   a. looking for food together / have enough to eat
   b. being together / survive

5. If emotional expression was instinctive for early humans, people from around the world _____ each other's emotional expression.
   a. should understand
   b. will misunderstand

6. Ekman wanted to find people living in a very remote area because these people _____.
   a. had a very different way of expressing emotions from those in Ekman's culture
   b. will not have been in touch with people from other places or learned emotional expression from them

7. Ekman found that people usually understand _____.
   a. all facial expressions from other cultures
   b. some facial expressions from other cultures, but not all

8. *Display rules* are rules in different cultures about _____.
   a. when to express emotion
   b. facial expressions and body language

9. _____ are more often learned, and _____ are often instinctive
   a. Facial expressions / gestures
   b. Gestures / facial expressions

2. ⌒ *Work with a partner. Fill in the middle column in the chart with information from the reading on pages 79–80. Then listen to the lecture again and complete the right-hand column with information you hear.*

Ideas	What the Reading Said	What the Professor Said
Body movements associated with fear		
Examples of how emotions helped early humans to survive		

(continued on next page)

Ideas	What the Reading Said	What the Professor Said
Evidence that the way we express some emotions is built into our biology		
Expressions of emotion that come from learning		

3. *In this exercise, you will prepare a three-minute talk to summarize the answer to one of the questions. Your talk will include a synthesis of ideas from the reading and the lecture. Follow the steps to prepare your talk.*

Step 1: Divide the class into two groups, Group A and Group B. Work with a partner from your group. Read your group's question.

> **Group A:** What evidence suggests that emotions are built into our biology?

> **Group B:** What evidence suggests that we learn how to express emotions?

Step 2: Look again at the chart in Exercise 2 on pages 85–86. Together, choose the most important information for your question.

Step 3: Use this information to make notes to talk from.

Step 4: Practice your talk with your partner.

Step 5: Work with a member of the opposite group. Take turns giving your talks. Then discuss this question:

> How much do you think emotional expression comes from biology and/or from learning? Explain.

Checkpoint 2   PEARSON LONGMAN myacademicconnectionslab

4

Building Academic Writing Skills

In this section, you will practice writing summary statements and synthesizing information. Then you will write about emotions and emotional expression using information from the readings and the lecture in this unit.

For online assignments, go to

Before You Write

1. *Read the paragraph. The main idea is stated twice. Underline each one. Identify the topic sentence.*

Some emotional responses appear to be biologically "built in" to every human. Some of the evidence for this comes from research by Irenäus Eibl-Eibesfeldt. In the early '70s, he devised a natural experiment to test this hypothesis. His study included babies who had been blind since birth. He watched their emotional expressions over the first few months of their life. It was clear that they smiled, frowned, and cried just like other children. Clearly they could not have learned these responses by watching their parents, because they could not see them. Thus, it is clear that these responses are biological, not learned from other people.

Source: Adapted from Zimbardo, P., Johnson, R. L., Weber, A. L., & Gruber, C. W. (2007). *Psychology, AP Edition.* Upper Saddle River, NJ: Pearson Prentice Hall.

Writing Summary Statements in Paragraphs

Many paragraphs have a statement at the end, which summarizes the main idea. It is often a good idea to include a summary statement because it helps to make the main idea clear. However, not all paragraphs have a summary statement. For example, they are not as useful for introductory paragraphs of essays or in short paragraphs. Only write summary statements where you think they are useful.

2. *Read the two paragraphs. Decide which one needs a summary statement most. Discuss your answer with a partner. Then write a summary statement for the paragraph you chose.*

Sample Paragraph 1

How many emotions are there? A long look at the dictionary turns up more than 500 emotional terms. Most experts, however, see a small number of basic emotions. Ekman lists six or seven, which you have already come across. Robert Plutchik's research suggests that there might be eight basic emotions. Plutchik's list is very similar to Ekman's. But what about emotions that are not on either list? One theory says that each emotion is a combination of the basic emotions. For example, disappointment is a mixture of sadness and surprise.

(continued on next page)

Sample Paragraph 2

Many animals display emotions in a similar way to humans. Chimpanzees and wolves both open their eyes wide when frightened, and so do humans. Also, human voices tend to be higher when we experience positive emotions such as happiness and lower when angry. Similarly, dogs generally have a higher pitched bark when playing with other dogs but a lower-pitched bark when angry or afraid.

3. *Write a paragraph with a summary statement to answer the question. Use ideas from the reading on pages 79–80.*

Some emotional responses are built into our biology. We learn others. What are some ways we learn some emotional responses? Give examples.

Focused Writing

Synthesizing Information in Writing

One process for synthesizing information in writing is similar to summarizing, which you learned about in Unit 4.
1. List the ideas from each text, lecture, or source that might be relevant.
2. Mark the ideas that are most relevant.
3. Move the ideas around so that they follow a logical order.
4. Write a first draft.
5. Check that your first draft has a clear main idea expressed in a topic sentence and perhaps a summary statement, is cohesive, summarizes well, and shows the relationships between the ideas.
6. Write your second draft.

You are going to practice synthesizing information by writing a paragraph that answers this question: **What happens when someone is frightened?** *Use information from the reading on pages 79–80, the lecture, and Figure 5.1 on page 77. Follow the steps.*

Step 1: In your notebook, draw a chart similar to the one you completed on pages 85–86 to help you collect information. Then complete your chart.

Step 2: Compare your chart with another student's, and make any necessary changes.

Step 3: Underline the ideas that are most relevant to the question.

Step 4: Organize your ideas. Number the ideas in a systematic order.

Step 5: Write a first draft of your paragraph.

Step 6: Work with a partner. Exchange your paragraphs. Comment on each other's paragraphs. Check that your partner's paragraph:

- ❏ has a clear main idea expressed in a topic sentence.
- ❏ has a summary statement if necessary.
- ❏ is cohesive.
- ❏ summarizes well.
- ❏ shows clear relationship between ideas.

Step 7: Revise your paragraph if necessary.

Integrated Writing Task

You have read texts and listened to a lecture about emotions. You will now use your knowledge of the content, vocabulary, and synthesizing skills to write one or two paragraphs or a short academic essay to answer this question: **Where do our emotional responses come from: Learning, biology, or both?** Your writing should include topic sentences, cohesion, and summary statements.

Follow the steps to write your paragraphs.

Step 1: Look back at the chart you completed in Focused Listening on pages 85–86. Underline the ideas that could be useful for your task.

Step 2: Reread the paragraphs in Before You Write on pages 87–88. Underline any ideas that are useful.

Step 3: Use the diagram to help you organize your ideas.

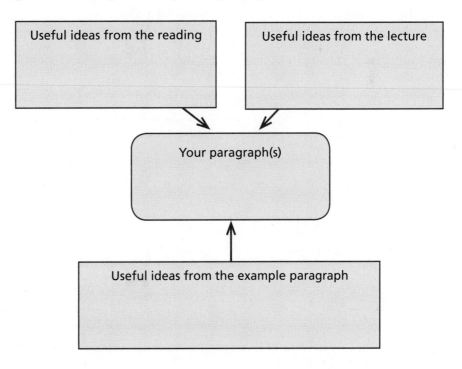

Step 4: Write a first draft.

Step 5: Work with a partner. Exchange your first drafts. Comment on each other's work. Use the checklist.

The paragraph . . .	Yes
has a clear main idea expressed in a topic sentence.	
has a summary statement if necessary.	
is cohesive.	
summarizes well.	
shows clear relationship between ideas.	

Step 6: Based on your discussion with your partner, write a final draft and give it to your teacher.

UNIT 6

Sociology
The Effects of Prosperity

Unit Description

Content: This course is designed to familiarize the student with concepts in sociology.

Skills: Fact and Opinion

- Identifying and evaluating information presented to support a position
- Recognizing a speaker's degree of certainty
- Distinguishing between facts and opinions
- Discussing opinions and supporting ideas
- Supporting opinions

Unit Requirements

Lecture: "It Is the Best of Times"

Readings: "It Is the Worst of Times" (an excerpt from an academic journal)
"Bhutan" (an excerpt from a TV news show)

Listening: "Student discussion"

Integrated Speaking Task: Discussing an issue of prosperity versus happiness

Assignments: www.MyAcademicConnectionsLab.com

1

Preview

For online assignments, go to

myacademicconnectionslab

Key Words

GDP *n* (Gross Domestic Product) the money that a country produces in a year

life expectancy *n* the number of years people live, on average

literacy rate *n* the percentage of people who can read and write

mental health *n* the health of a person's mind

per capita *adj* for each person

population *n* number of people in a country, city, or area

social *adj* connected with people in general; **society** *n*

statistic *n* a number that shows some information

wealth *n* the amount of money a country or person owns

Previewing the Academic Content

In many countries, life seems to be easier now than at any time in history. We have wonderful technology that helps us to do things that our grandparents could only dream about. Most countries have more wealth than ever before. But is this all good? Many people argue that there are problems. Statistics show that many countries have worse social problems as they get richer. So, is it really the best of times? In this unit, you will hear ideas from both sides of this discussion. Then you can make up your own mind!

Work with a partner. Look at the statistics in the chart. Then answer the questions.

	Country A	Country B
Population[1]	5,460,000	657,000
GDP per capita[2]	$56,427	$1,668
Life expectancy[3]	78	55
Literacy rate[4]	99%	47%

Sources: [1] World Bank for 2007
[2] World Bank for 2007
[3] CIA World Factbook, 2007
[4] UN Development Program Report 2007/2008

1. Based on the information in the chart, which country would you prefer to live in? Why?

2. What do you think life is like in these two countries? You can talk about:
   - going shopping
   - technology
   - happiness
   - chances to go to college
   - other _____

   Example

   People in Country A probably go shopping more than people in Country B because they have more money.

3. Which factors do you think are important for happiness? Choose the three most important to you. Explain your choices.
   - wealth
   - good physical health
   - good mental health
   - family and/or friends
   - a good job
   - appliances to make life easier, such as dishwashers and cars
   - opportunities to buy almost anything you want

4. Do you think your life is better than the life of your grandparents? Explain.

Previewing the Academic Skills Focus

In this unit, you will practice distinguishing between facts and opinions. You will also practice recognizing a speaker's degree of certainty, identifying and evaluating information, and expressing and justifying your opinion about an issue or preference.

1. *Look at the questions. Think about possible answers. Which question has an answer that can't be questioned easily? Which question has an answer about which people might disagree?*

   1. Which has a larger population, Bhutan or Denmark?
   2. In which country is it more enjoyable to live, Bhutan or Denmark?

Statements can be **facts** or **opinions**.

- **Facts** have evidence that is difficult to question. In other words, it can be tested or proven. People generally agree about facts.
- **Opinions** are a person's thoughts, beliefs, or feelings about something. Opinions are often introduced by phrases such as: *I think (that), I believe (that), In my opinion, It seems to me (that),* etc. In other words, opinions have evidence or information that can be questioned more easily.

To help you decide if a statement is a fact or an opinion, ask yourself these questions:

- Can I check whether it is true?
- Would other people have a different opinion about it?

2. *Work with a partner. Use the two questions in the skill box to decide if the statements are facts or opinions. Write **F** (fact) or **O** (opinion).*

_____ 1. According to the World Bank, the population of Denmark in 2007 was 5,460,000.[1]

_____ 2. The Brazilian soccer team is the best in the world.

_____ 3. Brazil is the most successful team in the history of the soccer World Cup. They have won five times, which is more than any other country.

_____ 4. Green tea ice cream tastes good.

_____ 5. Surveys by the Japan Ice Cream Association show that green tea is the third most popular flavor of ice cream in Japan.[2]

Source: [1]CIA World Factbook, 2007;
[2]http://www.icecream.or.jp/data/hakusho01.html

Before You Listen

1. *Read the paragraph. Then work in small groups. Answer the questions.*

1. What do people of your grandparents' generation say about the old days?

2. Which of the points in the paragraph would they agree with? For example, would they agree that life was simpler in the past?

3. Was there a "golden age" in your country? When was it?

Some people believe that there was a "golden age" in the past. They believe that there was a time when life was simple and pure, with fewer problems than modern life. It is true that there was less technology, life was less convenient, and people's disposable incomes were probably much less than now. However, people were happier, they respected each other, families were closer, and people lived together peacefully. For those who believe in the golden age, people who lived in those times were fortunate.

2
Building Academic Listening Skills

In this section, you will practice evaluating ideas and arguments. You will also practice recognizing a speaker's degree of certainty about the statements he or she makes.

For online assignments, go to

PEARSON LONGMAN
myacademicconnectionslab

Key Words

decrease *v* to become smaller

disposable income *n* the amount of money someone can spend on things they want but don't actually need

double(d) *adj* two times (200%) as big

fortunate *adj* happening because of good luck

halve *v* to become half (50%) as big

income *n* the money a person regularly receives, usually from doing a job

triple(d) *adj* three times (300%) as big

twice *adv* two times; *twice as much* means two times as much

2. *Work with a partner. Make some guesses about the statements. Use the key words to complete the sentences.*

In the United States,

1. the population is _____ what it was in 1945.

2. farmers and food companies produce _____ the amount of food, compared with 1945.

3. the number of deaths in road traffic accidents _____ between 1980 and 2006.

4. people are _____ because they can buy more than _____ as much with their _____ today compared with the mid-1950s.

Global Listening

1. 🎧 *Read the questions in the chart. Then listen to the lecture. Answers to these questions represent the lecturer's opinions, and they are the main ideas of the lecture. Write them in the chart. Then compare your chart with a partner's.*

Question	Lecturer's Opinions (Main Ideas)
1. Is life more convenient now than in the past?	
2. Can people buy more now than in the past?	
3. Are we safer now than in the past?	
4. Would modern people find it easy to live as people did in 1900?	
5. Did a "golden age" exist?	
6. Overall, in the last 100 years, which was the best time: 1900, the 1950s, or now?	

 Unit 6 ■ The Effects of Prosperity   **95**

2. *Work with a partner. Discuss the questions.*

1. Does the lecturer feel fortunate all the time, or just some of the time? How do you know?

2. What do you think the lecturer will talk about next?

Focused Listening

1. 🎧 *Listen to the lecture again and write notes about the details in the Supporting Details column in the chart. Then compare your notes with a partner's.*

Main Ideas	Supporting Details
1. Life is more convenient now than in the past.	
2. People can buy more now than in the past.	
3. People are safer now than in the past.	
4. Modern people would find it difficult to live as people did in 1900.	
5. A "Golden Age" did not exist in the past.	
6. Now is the best time in the last 100 years.	

2. *Use your notes to check your answers in Exercise 2 in the Before You Listen section on page 95.*

Ideas and arguments presented to support a position can be strong or weak. In academic situations, it is important to see the difference between strong and weak support. Look for strong support. This is an important part of critical thinking.

Usually, **strong ideas and arguments**:
- are based on facts
- are based on clear logic

Weak ideas and arguments are often:
- based on opinions
- based on statements that look like facts but that have no supporting evidence or reference
- based on only one example, which might not be usual or normal

3. Work with a partner. Discuss the strength of the main ideas you heard in the lecture and complete the chart. Overall, do you think the lecturer's opinions are well supported? Write your reasons in the chart.

Main Idea	How Strong Is the Evidence?	Reason
1. Life is more convenient now than in the past.		
2. People can buy more now than in the past.		
3. People are safer now than in the past.		

(continued on next page)

Unit 6 ■ The Effects of Prosperity   **97**

Main Idea	How Strong Is the Evidence?	Reason
4. Modern people would find it difficult to live as people did in 1900.		
5. A "Golden Age" did not exist in the past.		
6. Now is the best time in the last 100 years.		

Recognizing a Speaker's Degree of Certainty

Speakers use various words and expressions to show how certain they are about their ideas and points. For example, if someone says, *People are certainly wealthier now than their grandparents were,* they are expressing that they are sure about this point. Be careful, though—just because someone shows he or she is certain about something through his or her choice of words, it doesn't mean he or she is talking about a fact.

4. *Work with a partner. Place the words from the box on the scale on page 99.*

~~certainly~~	definitely	is	maybe	not sure	probably
could	doubtless	likely	might	perhaps	

not at
all certain

somewhat
certain

certain
certainly

5. 🎧 *Listen to some statements from the lecture. Write the number of the statement on the scale.*

not at
all certain

somewhat
certain

certain

Before You Read

1. *Work in small groups. Look at the bar graph. It shows some social trends from the text you will read. Guess where the words from the box go on the graph. Write them on the lines.*

3

Building Academic Reading Skills

In this section, you will practice distinguishing facts from opinions and evaluating information presented to support a position.

For online assignments, go to

PEARSON LONGMAN myacademicconnectionslab

| depression | divorce | teenage suicide | violent crime |

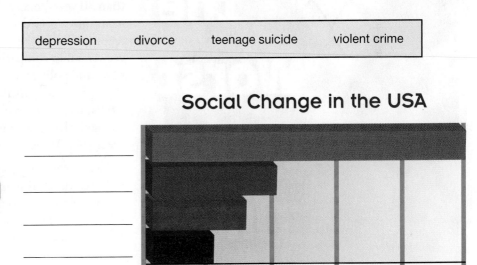

Social Change in the USA

0   2   4   6   8   10

Times increase since 1960
(since 1930, in the case of depression)

commit suicide v to kill oneself

crime n breaking the law; **criminal** adj

depression n a mental illness in which you feel very unhappy; **depressed** adj

divorce v to end a marriage; **divorce** n

increase v to add more to size or number; **increase** n

trend n a general change over a period of time

violent adj trying to injure or kill; **violence** n

2. *What feeling do you get from the statistics in the graph on page 99? How does that feeling compare with the lecturer's feeling? Discuss in small groups.*

3. *Think about your own country. Are these problems increasing, decreasing, or staying about the same? Discuss in small groups. Use the words for degrees of certainty on page 98.*

Global Reading

Skim the reading. Write the paragraph number next to each main idea. Then compare your answers with a partner's. Discuss what clues in the text helped you choose your answers.

_____ Index of National Civic Health

_____ Children and young people

_____ The forces behind the social changes

_____ Behind the numbers are real people

_____ Social problems

It Is the Worst of Times

by David G. Myers
(from "The Best of Times, the Worst of Times.")

1 We earn more money, we eat better food, we live in better houses, we have better education, and we are healthier than ever before. We also have faster communication and more convenient transportation. However, for more than 30 years, many developed countries went into a very deep social recession.[1] This recession made the economic recessions look very small in comparison, even though our news and politics focused on the economy. If you fell asleep in 1960 and woke up in the 1990s, would you feel pleased with the cultural change? Here are some other facts that would greet you. As we will see, since 1960:

- Twice as many people are getting divorced.
- Three times as many teenagers are committing suicide.
- There are four times as many violent crimes.
- Five times as many people are in prison.
- Up to ten times more people suffer from depression now than in the 1930s.

---

[1] **recession** n decline, slowing down

per Person Income
(1995 dollars)

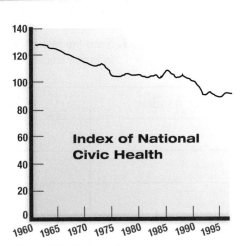

Index of National
Civic Health

2 The National Commission on Civic Renewal put together trends such as these in an index. This index is called the "Index of National Civic Health." It has fallen steadily since 1960. These figures are for the United States, but many other Western countries have experienced similar trends.

3 Behind these numbers, this index, are real people with real problems. As Bertrand Russell once said, a person is civilized[2] when he or she can look at some statistics and cry. Can we cry for all the damaged lives behind these numbers? We have more material goods than ever before, but there are also more people with emptiness in their lives.

4 At the center of the social recession are children and young people. Elizabeth Gilman and Yale University psychologist Edward Zigler found that other researchers agree with each other about this. They looked at statistics for child well-being over the last 30 years. They found that the current statistics were the worst ever. Urie Bronfenbrenner, a respected psychologist, described the trends simply. She said that the situation of children and families in the United States is the greatest internal problem in the country's history. American Psychological Association president Martin Seligman was struck by an interesting fact: He said that every statistic about the material well-being of young Americans is getting better, but that every statistic about their mental well-being is getting worse.

5 Can we make the negative social forces clear to people, and then renew our society? And what are the negative forces? How can things have gone so well materially and so poor socially? In other words, these are not the best of times. Robert Frank, an economist at Cornell University, notes that North Americans are spending more hours at work, fewer hours sleeping, and fewer hours with friends and family. Roads are much more busy, people are saving much less money and feeling worried that their jobs might disappear. Similar patterns are happening in other developed countries—in Europe, Australia, and Japan.

---

[2] **civilized** *adj* polite and reasonable, suited to modern, well-organized society

Source: Adapted from Myers, D.G. (2001). The best of times, the worst of times. In *The American paradox: Spiritual hunger in an age of plenty* (pp. 1–12). New Haven, CT: Yale University Press.

Focused Reading

1. *Scan the text to find five social trends. Complete the left-hand column. Then read in detail where these trends are mentioned and complete the rest of the chart.*

Social Trends	How Big Was the Change?

2. *Use the text to answer the questions. Circle the correct answer.*

1. Which is closest to the meaning of *recession* in this sentence from paragraph 1: "However, for more than 30 years, many developed countries went into a very deep social recession"?
   a. a time when the economy has problems
   b. a time when problems develop
   c. a time when more people take a break from study or work

2. What does the author mean in paragraph 3 when he writes, "We have more material goods than ever before"?
   a. People in the United States have more clothes.
   b. The United States makes more clothes.
   c. People in the United States are wealthier.

3. What is a good conclusion to draw from the two graphs in reading?
   a. People are getting richer and happier.
   b. People are getting richer but are having other problems.
   c. People are getting richer but less healthy.

4. In paragraph 3, what did Bertrand Russell mean?
   a. Civilized people get very emotional when they see numbers.
   b. Civilized people don't think that statistics help to solve problems.
   c. Civilized people can clearly imagine what numbers really mean.

5. Which is the best interpretation of these sentences from paragraph 4: "They looked at statistics for child well-being over the last 30 years. They found that the current statistics were the worst ever"?
   a. Children were in a better situation 30 years ago than now.
   b. Children were in a worse situation 30 years ago than now.
   c. Children are suffering less from disease now, compared with 30 years ago.

6. Which sentence best represents the author's opinion in the last paragraph?
   a. The social problems could be caused by too much focus on work.
   b. People aren't enjoying themselves enough.
   c. Social problems mean that now is not the best of times; the past was better.

Distinguishing between Facts and Opinions

As we saw earlier, people don't always show directly whether a point is a fact or opinion. Instead, you have to ask questions based on your understanding of the whole text:

- Does the author give evidence supporting his/her point?
- Is it possible to check evidence for the point, in other sources such as books, journals, or very reliable internet sites?
- How likely are other people to have different opinions about it?

3. *The sentences in the chart are from the reading. Work with a partner. For each point in the chart:*
- underline the evidence for the point in the reading
- complete the second and third column in the chart
- use the information in the second and third column to decide whether the points are fact or opinion and complete the fourth column

Point Made in Reading	Can You Check the Supporting Evidence? Why (not)?	How Likely are Other People to Have Different Opinions About It?	Fact or Opinion?
Paragraph 1: we . . . have . . . more convenient transportation.			
Paragraph 1: for more than 30 years, many developed countries went into a very deep social recession.			
Paragraph 1: This recession made the economic recessions look very small in comparison.			

(continued on next page)

 Unit 6 ■ The Effects of Prosperity **103**

Point Made in Reading	Can You Check the Supporting Evidence? Why (not)?	How Likely are Other People to Have Different Opinions About It?	Fact or Opinion?
Paragraph 3: Behind these numbers, this index, are real people with real problems.			
Paragraph 4: At the center of the social recession are children and young people.			
Paragraph 4: Martin Seligman was struck by an interesting fact: He said that every statistic about the material well-being of young Americans is getting better, but that every statistic about their mental well-being is getting worse.			
Paragraph 5: North Americans are spending more hours at work, fewer hours sleeping, and fewer hours with friends and family.			

4. *Work in small groups. Discuss the questions.*

1. Overall, how certain is the author of the reading about his opinions? Can you find any evidence of uncertainty?

2. Some people say that growing up with just one parent can be just as good as having both parents at home. Do you think the author would agree with this statement? Do you agree with this statement? Why or why not?

3. What were the most surprising, interesting, or unpleasant things you heard in the lecture or found in the reading?

4. Which opinions do you disagree with? Why?

5. Which opinions do you agree with? Why?

5. *Write a short paragraph that tells what the lecture and the reading say about mental and physical health. Follow the steps.*

Step 1: Review the lecture and reading. Take notes about what each says about mental and physical health. Compare your notes with a partner's.

Step 2: Plan and write your paragraph. Think about the strategies you learned in previous units for synthesizing information, topic sentences, supporting ideas, summary sentences, and relationship words.

Step 3: Work with a partner. Read your partner's paragraph. Underline the facts in one color and the opinions in another.

Checkpoint 2   PEARSON LONGMAN **myacademicconnectionslab**

Before You Speak

Discussing Opinions and Supporting Ideas

At the university level, you will often have to participate in discussions. These may happen when lectures are small. Also, depending on the university, you may have extra sessions in which this happens. These sessions may be called "seminars," "recitations," or "tutorials." In these, you may be given a mark for your participation in discussions. Thus, it is important to practice discussing opinions and giving supporting ideas and evidence.

To give an opinion, you can use these expressions:
- *I think/believe/feel (that) . . .*
- *It is my opinion (that) . . .*
- *In my opinion, . . .*
- *It seems to me that . . .*

To support an opinion, you can use these expressions:
- *. . . because . . .*
- *. . . for several reasons . . .*
- *. . . for the reason that . . .*

To show agreement with an opinion, you can use these expressions:
- *I think so, too.*
- *I agree (with you).*
- *I feel the same way.*
- *(I think) you're right.*

To show disagreement with an opinion, you can use these expressions:
- *I see what you mean, but. . .*
- *I disagree (with you).*
- *Yes, but . . .*
- *Actually, . . .*
- *I don't/can't agree (with you).*

1. *You will hear a discussion between students about a documentary. Before you listen, read the short description of the country they will talk about.*

Bhutan

Bhutan is a small country located in the Himalaya mountains between India and Tibet. In 1972, King Jigme Singye Wangchuck declared that Gross National Happiness was more important for his country than Gross Domestic Product. Since then, the government has used GNH ideas to guide the country's development. From the statistics, though, many may think the country has problems. According to the CIA's *The World Factbook* (2007), it is one of the world's "least developed" countries. The economy is based mostly on subsistence farming,[1] and the 2007 estimated per capita GDP was only around U.S.$2,000. Television was only introduced in 1999, and by 2006 there were only 31,500 telephone lines connecting the population of just over 680,000. However, Gross National Happiness policies seem to be working. In 2006, research by Leicester University in the UK published in *Business Week* magazine, ranked Bhutan the happiest country in Asia and the eighth happiest country in the world. So perhaps money, modern conveniences, and consumerism aren't the road to happiness that some people might think!

---

[1] **subsistence farming** *n* farming that produces just enough food for the farmer to live, without extra for sale

Bhutan. (2007). *The world factbook.* Washington DC: Central Intelligence Agency.
The world's happiest countries. (2006). *Business Week.* Retrieved May 14, 2009, from http://images.businessweek.com/ss/06/10/happiest_countries/index_01.htm.

2. *Work with a partner. Discuss the questions.*

1. What are the advantages of living in Bhutan?

2. What are the disadvantages of living there?

3. 🎧 *Listen to the discussion. Write expressions used by the speakers in the first row of the chart.*

	Agreeing with Someone	Partly Agreeing	Disagreeing	Showing Understanding
Expressions in the discussion	Yes, it looks as though it is. . .			
Other expressions with the same meaning				

4. *In the second row in the chart, write other expressions you know that have the same meaning or use. Compare your chart with a partner's.*

Focused Speaking

Supporting Opinions

When you give your opinion in a presentation (or an essay), it is important to support your opinion with evidence. Strong support will help people believe your opinion.

Strong support could include:
- facts, such as research results and statistics
- a clear and logical explanation or reason, based on facts

Weak support might be:
- another opinion
- facts that people can't check easily

Make sure your ideas are specific, logical, and clear. In addition, use words that show a strong level of certainty.

1. 🎧 *Listen again to the discussion. After each person gives an opinion, write what kind of supporting evidence he or she gives. More than one answer is possible. Then discuss your answers with a partner.*

Kind of Supporting Evidence
- facts, such as research results
- an explanation or reason
- another opinion
- facts that can't be checked easily

PROFESSOR: ". . . money doesn't always buy happiness . . ."

STUDENT 1: [agrees with the professor] _____

STUDENT 2: [disagrees with the professor] _____

STUDENT 3: ". . . there's a problem with these surveys" _____

STUDENT 2: [disagrees with student 3] _____

STUDENT 1: ". . . make sure there isn't a big gap between wealthy people and

poor people" _____

2. *Work with a partner. Do you think the evidence the students use is strong or weak? Why?*

STUDENT 1: _____

STUDENT 2: _____

3. *Read the questions and think about your answers. For each question, decide your opinion and think of support for your opinion. Try to make the support strong. You may take notes if you need to.*
- How much would you like to live a Bhutanese lifestyle?
- Do you think Gross National Happiness is a good idea? Why or why not?
- Is it possible to be happy without modern technology? Why or why not?

4. *Work with a partner to discuss the questions.*

Integrated Speaking Task

You have listened to a lecture and read texts about prosperity and happiness. You will now use your knowledge of the content, vocabulary, degrees of certainty, and facts vs. opinions to have a discussion with two or three other students about this question: **Does prosperity lead to happiness?**

In your discussion, use:
- ideas from the main reading, lecture, and news story about Bhutan
- your own opinions, with supporting strong evidence
- expressions for discussions

Follow the steps to prepare for your discussion.

Step 1: Prepare what you are going to say about the topic. Remember to include supporting evidence. Use the chart to organize your ideas.

Main Ideas	Supporting Details (evidence)

Step 2: Work in groups of three or four students. Choose a discussion leader. This person's job is to start the discussion by asking the discussion question, and to make sure everyone has a turn at speaking.

Step 3: Have the discussion. While you listen, take notes in your notebooks on what you hear. You can use a chart like the one in Step 1.

Step 4: Discussion leaders from each group will summarize for the class the points their group made. Group members will assist the leader and help answer questions from other groups.

Step 5: Discuss the questions with the class.

1. Which group made the highest number of unique points?

2. Which two points had the strongest supporting evidence based on facts?

3. What are two points that didn't have strong supporting evidence based on facts?

Literature
CHINUA ACHEBE

Unit Description

Content: This course is designed to familiarize the student with the life and works of the writer Chinua Achebe.

Skills: Purpose

- Recognizing a speaker's attitude
- Recognizing multiple purposes in texts
- Writing introductions and conclusions in essays
- Considering your audience

Unit Requirements

Lecture: "Background on Chinua Achebe"

Reading: Excerpt from *Marriage Is a Private Affair* (from *Girls at War and Other Stories* by Chinua Achebe)

Listening: *Marriage Is a Private Affair* (a summary)

Integrated Writing Task: Writing an academic essay about *Marriage Is a Private Affair*

Assignments:
www.MyAcademicConnectionsLab.com

1

Preview

For online assignments, go to

For online assignments, go to

Key Words

background *n* the situation and past events that help the audience to understand a story

character *n* the personal qualities and personality of one of the people in a novel, play, or short story

develop *v* to become more advanced (i.e., your knowledge of a story or character develops)

Previewing the Academic Content

Chinua Achebe, from Nigeria, is one of the most famous African writers. Much of his work is about his home region, which has changed drastically in his lifetime. Many of his stories are about the effects of this change on the local culture—something that is also happening to many other societies around the world.

In this unit, you will hear a lecture about the author and read part of a short story that he wrote called *Marriage Is a Private Affair*.

1. *Work with a partner. Match the pictures to the words in the box. Write the correct words under the pictures.*

| novel | play | poem |

a. _____   b. _____   c. _____

2. *Think of a novel, poem, or play you have read or watched. Complete the middle column of the chart. Then work with a partner. Use the ideas in the left-hand column of the chart to ask your partner questions. Write notes about your partner's answers. Use the key words.*

	Your Novel, Poem, or Play	Your Partner's Novel, Poem, or Play
Title		
The main characters		
Background information		

	Your Novel, Poem, or Play	Your Partner's Novel, Poem, or Play
Events that helped the story develop		
Changes the character went through during the story		

In this unit, you will practice identifying a writer or speaker's purpose and attitude.

Previewing the Academic Skills Focus

1. *Why do you think people write novels, plays, and poems, such as the ones you talked about? Work with a partner to discuss the question.*

Purpose

Purpose is what the speaker or writer wants to accomplish with the text; it is the reason behind a spoken or written text.

Some common purposes are:
- to persuade—to make others believe an opinion or point of view
- to inform—to give information
- to explain—to tell how and why
- to narrate—to tell a story
- to entertain—to amuse or interest others

To understand a text well, it is important to understand the writer or speaker's purpose—why the text was written. This is an important part of critical thinking.

2. *Match the text types on the left with their purposes on the right. Each text type may have more than one purpose. Compare your answers with a partner's.*

_____ 1. a university lecture about a novel

_____ 2. conversation between students about the poem

_____ 3. a newspaper review of a play

_____ 4. an encyclopedia entry about an author

_____ 5. an academic debate

a. to tell people whether it is good or not

b. to make others agree with an opinion

c. to give information to ordinary people

d. to build friendship

e. to give information to students

3. *Work with a partner. Discuss the possible purposes for each item. Think of more than one purpse for each.*

1. an advertisement for a play

2. a student's notes, taken during a literature lecture

3. a student essay

Before You Listen

1. *Read the encyclopedia entry about Chinua Achebe.*

Chinua Achebe
(pronounced: /ˈtʃɪnwɑː əˈtʃɛbeɪ) is a novelist and poet from Nigeria. His first novel, *Things Fall Apart,* is one of the most famous and widely read African novels. Achebe was born in 1930, when Nigeria was still a British colony. His early experiences have been a major influence on his work and provide many of the themes in his stories. Christian missionaries from Britain were very active in the part of Nigeria where he grew up. As a result, many people of his generation and older grew up with a mixture of the local religion and Christianity.

Key Words

colony *n*
generation *n*
influence *n*
missionary *n*
religion *n*
theme *n*

2. *Find the words in the biography of Chinua Achebe. Determine their meaning from the context. Write the words next to their definitions.*

1. _____ all the people who were born at around the same time

2. _____ a belief in one or more gods, and the behaviors that go with this belief (e.g., going to a special building on a certain day of the week)

3. _____ a topic that we see several times in a piece of literature

4. _____ a country or area that is controlled by another country

5. _____ someone who goes to another country and tries to make people believe his or her religion

6. _____ have an effect on something

Global Listening

1. 🎧 *Read the names in the box. Then listen to the pronunciation of each one.*

Igbo	the group of people in Nigeria, from whom Achebe comes
Portugal	a country in Europe
Nnaemeka	the main male character in the story
Nene	the main female character in the story
Lagos	a big city in Nigeria; at the time of this story it was the capital of Nigeria

2. 🎧 *Work in groups of three. Listen to the lecture. Each group member should focus on one main point, and write the answers on a separate piece of paper. Then exchange your answers.*

STUDENT A: What does the professor say about Achebe?

STUDENT B: What does the professor say about Nigeria and Lagos?

STUDENT C: What does the professor say about the story, *Marriage Is a Private Affair?*

Focused Listening

1. 🎧 *Would the professor agree with the following statements? Listen to the lecture again. Write **A** (agree), **D** (disagree), or **N** (no information in the lecture). Explain your answers in your notebook. Then compare your answers with a partner's. Discuss any differences.*

  A   1. Understanding background information can help you understand literature.

The answer is A (agree) because the professor said, "let's have a little look at some of the background. That will help you to understand the story."

_____ 2. Achebe's writing has little connection with tradition.

_____ 3. Arranged marriages are good.

_____ 4. Among Christians around the world nowadays, arranged marriages are not common.

_____ 5. Everyone in the cities understands the traditional cultures well.

2. *Work with a partner. What kind of feeling does each statement express? Write the number of each statement on the scale.*

1. It's a good novel.

2. It's a very interesting novel.

3. It's nothing special.

4. I found it hard to finish.

5. It was really fascinating.

←————————————————————————————————————→

NEGATIVE   NEUTRAL   POSITIVE

Recognizing a Speaker's Attitude

The **speaker's attitude** is the speaker's feeling about the topic and/or about the listener.

One way to recognize a speaker's attitude is to listen for the specific words that are used.

Speaker's intonation (the way the voice goes up and down) is another way to express attitude. Strong intonation (going up and down a lot) indicates strong feelings—positive or negative. Flat intonation suggests more neutral feeling. Speakers can also show the strength of their feelings by giving words strong stress. They can pronounce the word more loudly, for longer, and with stronger intonation than the words around it.

3. ⌒ *Listen to the lecture again. What is the professor's attitude about these points? Place the number of each of her points on the scale. Take notes to help you explain your answers. Then discuss your answers with a partner.*

1. the novel, *Things Fall Apart*

2. connections between old traditions and new ideas

3. similarities with other countries

4. being diverse and complex

5. handing work in late

Lagos

←————————————————————————————————————→

NEGATIVE   NEUTRAL   POSITIVE

4. ⌒ *Listen to the excerpts from the lecture. In each excerpt, underline the word that is stressed most strongly. Compare your answers with a partner's.*

1. Some say it is the most popular African novel, . . .

2. These changes have resulted in some fascinating connections, . . .

3. Must be a fascinating place!

4. I don't want a repeat of last month's problems with lateness.

5. *Which example do you think best expresses the speaker's purpose in giving the lecture? Discuss your answer with the class.*

- to help students understand what they are going to read
- to make students laugh
- to persuade the students that her opinions are correct
- to make students more interested in African literature

3
Building Academic Reading Skills

In this section, you will practice recognizing purpose in texts.
For online assignments, go to

PEARSON LONGMAN
myacademicconnectionslab

Before You Read

Some people say that this painting shows the relationship between the two characters as well as the mood of the story you are going to read. Look at the painting. Then discuss the questions with the class.

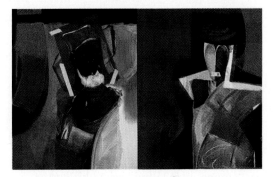

1. How are these two people feeling?

2. What feeling do you get from the picture—positive or negative?

3. What other adjectives can you use to describe the feeling of the picture?

4. What can you say about the relationship of the two people?

Key Words

atmosphere *n* the feeling that people get from being in a place

cosmopolitan *adj* having people from many cultures

determine *v* to choose

engagement *n* an agreement by two people to get married

fiancée *n* the woman a man is going to marry

tribe *n* a group of people with the same culture, customs, and beliefs and who come from the same place; not usually used when the people have their own country

Global Reading

1. *Read the introduction. Then take just three minutes to skim the story on pages 118–119.*

This text is an excerpt from a story *Marriage Is a Private Affair.* At the start of the story, Nnaemeka was talking with his fiancée, Nene. He was explaining why it is best to tell his father of their engagement in person, not by mail. Being a city girl, she has only experienced the modern way of life, and arranged marriage is not a part of that. She has trouble understanding how their relationship could upset Nnaemeka's father, and why a letter might not be the best way to break the news. As the story says, "in the cosmopolitan atmosphere of the city it had always seemed to her something of a joke that a person's tribe could determine whom he married." However, there was one thing Nnaemeka didn't tell Nene—shortly before this conversation, he had received a letter from his father. The letter told him about the future wife the father had chosen for him.

From

MARRIAGE IS A PRIVATE AFFAIR

by Chinua Achebe

On the second evening of his return from Lagos Nnaemeka sat with his father under a cassia tree. . . .

"Father," began Nnaemeka suddenly, "I have come to ask for forgiveness."

"Forgiveness? For what, my son?" he asked in amazement.

"It's about this marriage question."

"Which marriage question?"

"I can't—we must—I mean it is impossible for me to marry Nweke's daughter."

"Impossible? Why?" asked his father.

"I don't love her."

"Nobody said you did. Why should you?" he asked.

"Marriage today is different . . ."

"Look here, my son," interrupted his father, "nothing is different. What one looks for in a wife are a good character and a Christian background."

Nnaemeka saw there was no hope along the present line of argument.

"Moreover," he said, "I am engaged to marry another girl who has all of Ugoye's good qualities, and who . . ."

His father did not believe his ears. "What did you say?" he asked slowly and disconcertingly.[1]

"She is a good Christian," his son went on, "and a teacher in a Girls' School in Lagos."

"Teacher, did you say? If you consider that a qualification for a good wife I should like to point out to you, Nnaemeka, that no Christian woman should teach. St. Paul[2] . . . says that women should keep silence." He rose slowly from his seat and paced forwards and backwards. This was his pet subject, and he condemned vehemently those church leaders who encouraged women to teach in their schools. After he had spent his emotion on a long homily,[3] he at last came back to his son's engagement, in a seemingly milder tone.

"Whose daughter is she, anyway?"

"She is Nene Atang."

"What!" All the mildness was gone again. "Did you say Nene Atang, what does that mean?"

"Nene Atang from Calabar. She is the only girl I can marry." This was a very rash reply and Nnaemeka expected the storm to burst. But it did not. His father merely walked away into his room. This was most unexpected and perplexed Nnaemeka. His father's silence was infinitely more menacing than a flood of threatening speech. That night the old man did not eat.

When he sent for Nnaemeka a day later he applied all possible ways of dissuasion.[4] But the young man's heart was hardened, and his father eventually gave him up as lost.

---

[1] **disconcertingly** *adv* with worry and confusion

[2] **St. (Saint) Paul** was a very important person early in the history of Christianity.

[3] **homily** *n* a short speech given as a part of a Christian church ceremony; advice about how to behave that is often unwanted

[4] **dissuasion** *n* persuasion not to do something

"I owe it to you, my son, as a duty to show you what is right and what is wrong. Whoever put this idea into your head might as well have cut your throat. It is Satan's[5] work." He waved his son away.

"You will change your mind, Father, when you know Nene."

---

[5] **Satan** *n* evil spirit in Christianity
[6] **prayer** *n* message to a god

"I shall never see her," was the reply. From that night the father scarcely spoke to his son. He did not, however, cease hoping that he would realize how serious was the danger he was heading for. Day and night he put him in his prayers.[6]

2. *Put the events in the correct order. Then compare your answers with a partner's. Scan the text to check differences between your answers.*

_____ Nnaemeka explained why he can't marry Ugoye.

_____ Nnaemeka's father tried to persuade Nnaemeka to change his mind.

_____ Nnaemeka returned to his home village.

_1_ Nnaemeka received a letter from his father. The letter says that he should marry Ugoye.

_____ Nnaemeka's father became silent.

_____ Nnaemeka's father refused to ever see Nene.

_____ Nnaemeka and Nene discussed how to tell Nnaemeka's father about their engagement.

_____ Nnaemeka's father explained what is important in a wife.

_____ Nnaemeka told his father about Nene and her background.

Focused Reading

1. *Read the story again. Answer the questions. Write answers in your notebook. Then compare your answers with a partner's. Discuss the differences.*

1. According to the introduction you read on page 117, why will Nnaemeka's father be upset about his son's relationship with Nene?

2. Why do you think Nnaemeka didn't tell Nene about the letter from his father?

3. How do you know that Nnaemeka's father reacted strongly to the news about Nene?

4. What two things about Nene didn't Nnaemeka's father like?

5. Do you think Nnaemeka's father is stubborn[1]? Why?

6. Do you think Nnaemeka is stubborn? Why? Which part of the text supports your answer?

---

[1] **stubborn** *adj* refusing to change one's opinion even when this causes problems

A text can have more than one purpose—in fact, this is common. There is often a purpose that is clear on the surface, and there might also be a more hidden purpose. For example, on the surface, the purpose of an academic essay might be to put forward an opinion. But, if a student wrote the essay, the "hidden" purpose might be to get a good mark.

With literature, the "surface" purpose might be to tell a good story. The "hidden" purpose might be to inform people of social problems or to describe a society that the audience might not know about.

2. Work with a partner. Complete the chart for Marriage Is a Private Affair. Which of the purposes is the surface purpose? Which could be the hidden purpose? Write **S** or **H**. Explain your answers.

Text Purpose	Surface (S)/ Hidden (H)	Explanation
To give information		
To tell a story		
To inform the world about Nigerian society		
To entertain		
To show that the issues that people in Nigeria have to deal with are not so different from those in other countries		

3. *Work in small groups. Discuss the questions. Use the expressions for discussions from Unit 6 (page 105).*

1. Look back at the picture on page 117. Now that you've read part of the story, do you agree or disagree that the picture shows the relationship between the characters? Why?

2. The lecturer said "It's interesting to think about whether the same issues [about cultures changing] may happen in other countries that are also changing very quickly." Are there similar differences between adults and children's opinions in your country? What are they?

3. Think about the title. Does it fit best with the father's view of marriage or to Nene and Nnaemeka's? Why?

4. Could you imagine something similar happening to friends of yours? Why or why not?

5. Should children always obey their parents? Even adult children?

6. What should Nnaemeka do: Follow his father's wishes or his heart?

7. What do you think happens later in the story?

4. *Choose one person from your group to tell the class the main points from your discussion. Which group made the higest number of unique points?*

Checkpoint 2 PEARSON LONGMAN myacademicconnectionslab

Before You Write

1. *Read the question and the student essay that answers it.*

In what way is the life of the characters in *Marriage Is a Private Affair* similar to your life?

4
Building Academic Writing Skills

In this section, you will practice writing introductions and conclusions. Then you will write an essay about *Marriage Is a Private Affair* using information from the lecture and the readings in this unit.
For online assignments, go to

PEARSON LONGMAN myacademicconnectionslab

Although Achebe's writing is mostly about his home country, Nigeria, people around the world can relate to his themes. This is because his characters' experiences are similar to the experiences of all people who live in changing societies. One of his short stories, *Marriage Is a Private Affair*, shows this well. In particular, two themes are the same in my country and in the story: Differences of opinion between adults and children, and differences between the city and the countryside.

First, there is a difference in attitude between parents and children. For example, people from my country travel abroad more often than our parents did. Some people meet foreigners overseas and decide to get married. Some parents do not like this. However, just as the villagers' reactions in the story are complex, some parents are quite

(continued on next page)

happy with this. Certainly, clashes between older and younger people's attitudes do happen, though.

People in my country relate to another of Achebe's themes: Differences between cultures in the city and countryside. In the last 50 years, very many people have moved from the countryside to the city. Thus, many countryside traditions are lost. Like Nene in the story, younger people in the city have lost touch with the culture of the countryside. Thus, the culture of the country is changing, and this is causing confusion.

These are just two of the similarities between the life of the characters in Achebe's stories and my own country. I recommend that everyone read this story, because they might be able to relate the characters to their own lives and own country.

Writing Introductions and Conclusions in Essays

Earlier in this book, you learned how to write paragraphs. These might be part of the body of an essay. Well-written essays also have introductions and conclusions.

An **introduction** often consists of:
- a general statement, which introduces the topic
- a thesis statement, which gives an opinion. The body paragraphs support this opinion
- a scope, which gives a clue about the ideas that will follow in the body

Sometimes, these sections overlap.

A **conclusion** often consists of:
- a summary, which reminds the readers of the main ideas
- a recommendation, which suggests future action based on the thesis (only where appropriate)

2. Look at the introduction—the first paragraph—of the student essay on pages 121–122. Circle the general statement, thesis statement, and scope.

3. Look at the conclusion—the last paragraph. Circle the summary and recommendation.

Focused Writing

1. ⌒ Listen to a student giving a summary of the end of the story Marriage Is a Private Affair. Answer the questions.

1. Who is Okeke?

2. The speaker mentioned that Nnaemeka's neighbors had a variety of reactions. What reactions did he talk about in the summary?

3. What did Okeke think about sending Nnaemeka to a traditional doctor?

4. What did Okeke do with the photograph? Why?

5. How did Okeke feel about Nene's suggestion?

Considering Your Audience

The **audience** is the people who will read your writing or listen to you speak.

In planning what to write or say, it is important to think about your audience. Ask yourself these questions:

- What is interesting for the audience?
- What does the audience need to know?
- What does the audience know already?
- What is the audience's background? For example, how old are they?

With assignments in an academic setting, remember that the instructor is an audience. To get good marks on assignments, instructors usually need to see that you can:

- support your ideas with evidence (usually from readings or from lectures)
- synthesize ideas from the readings and lectures
- think critically about the ideas you read and heard
- find new ideas beyond those in the required reading and course lectures
- explain your points clearly

2. *Work with a partner. Think about the summary you listened to. Which questions might have been the most important for the speaker to think about? Number the questions in order of importance.*

_____ What is interesting for the audience?

_____ What does the audience need to know?

_____ What does the audience know already?

_____ What is the audience's background?

3. *Imagine you are going to give a presentation about the story,* Marriage Is a Private Affair, *to some other students. What background information would you give if:*

1. There have been no lectures or readings about African writers?

2. The students have had a lecture about Chinua Achebe and his novels, but not this story?

Use the questions in Exercise 2 to help you. Write your ideas in your notebook. Then share your ideas in small groups.

Integrated Writing Task

You have listened to a lecture about Nigerian life as it relates to Chinua Achebe and his writing, read an excerpt from *Marriage Is a Private Affair*, and heard a summary about it. You will now use your knowledge of the content, vocabulary, purpose, essay writing, and audience to write a four-paragraph essay in response to this question: **Clashes between the modern and the traditional have been an important theme both in Achebe's life and in his writing. What are some examples from *Marriage Is a Private Affair* that show this?**

Follow the steps to write your essay.

Step 1: Work in small groups. Complete the chart to organize ideas from the lecture, reading, and summary.

Differences between Traditional and More Modern Society		
Topics	Traditional (Okeke's generation)	More Modern (Nnaemeka and Nene's generation)
Marriage		
Religion		
Knowledge of traditions		
Women allowed to teach		

Step 2: Form new groups. Compare answers. Add the other students' ideas to your chart.

Step 3: Choose two topics to write about. Each topic will become a body paragraph.

Step 4: Plan your introduction. Use the skills box on page 122 to help you.

Step 5: Write the first draft of your essay. Remember the parts: introduction, body paragraphs, and conclusion.

Step 6: Check that your first draft has:
- the correct stages in the introduction, each body paragraph, and the conclusion
- the right amount of information for your audience

Step 7: Work with a partner. Exchange your essays. Comment on each other's essay. Use the checklist.

CHECKLIST	
Does the introduction have. . .	**Yes**
a general statement that introduces the topic?	
a thesis statement that gives the writer's opinion?	
a scope that gives a clue about the ideas that will follow in the body?	
Does each body paragraph support the opinion in the thesis statement?	
Does the conclusion have. . .	**Yes**
a summary of the main ideas?	
a recommendation?	

Step 8: Based on your discussion with your partner, write a final draft of your essay and give it to your teacher.

UNIT 8

Earth Science
The Water Cycle

Unit Description

Content: This course is designed to familiarize the student with concepts in earth science.

Skills: Inference
- Inferring meaning from context
- Drawing conclusions
- Inferring the speaker's purpose
- Using intonation to convey meaning
- Persuading your audience

Unit Requirements

Reading: "The Shrinking of the Aral Sea" (an excerpt from an environmental science textbook)

Lecture: "Human Intervention in the Water Cycle"

Listening: "Disappearing Rivers Threaten Food Supply" (a podcast)

Integrated Speaking Task: Giving a persuasive talk about human intervention in the water cycle

Assignments: www.MyAcademicConnectionsLab.com

1

Preview

For online assignments, go to

PEARSON LONGMAN
myacademicconnectionslab

Previewing the Academic Content

Water is extremely important for our lives—not just for drinking, but also for growing our food. Too much of it, and we have floods; too little, and we have drought. There is a natural cycle—the hydrologic cycle—that generally gives us the right amount of water. But if we disturb the cycle, disasters happen.

In this unit, we will look at some of these disasters and find out how they happened. From this, we will know how to avoid the same problems in the future.

1. Study the key words and the pictures. Then write the key words under the correct pictures.

a. _____   c. _____

b. _____

d. _____   e. _____

2. Work with a partner. Read an excerpt from a newspaper report. Discuss what consequences of the event might happen for:
- people who stay behind in their homes
- business owners
- farmers

STORM PREPARATIONS CONTINUE

People in Tai Zhou, China, are securing their homes and preparing to leave as the storm predicted for Friday night nears. Up to 15 inches (38 cm) of rain is expected, with winds of over 93 miles (150 km) per hour. It is expected to be several days before people can return to their homes.

Key Words

drought n a time when there is very little rain and growing food becomes difficult

dry up v to lose water or moisture over a period of time

erosion n damage caused by rain and wind on a natural surface; over time, erosion can cause areas of land to disappear or change shape; **erode** v

flood n water covering an area that is usually dry, such as houses or farm land

tropical cyclone n a very powerful storm, with very strong winds and heavy rain. Tropical storms that start in the Atlantic Ocean are called **hurricanes** and ones that start in the western Pacific, near East Asia, are called **typhoons**.

3. Complete the chart with natural disasters you have heard about on the news or read about in newspapers.

Type of Disaster	Country or Area	Result

4. Walk around the classroom. Ask other students about their charts. Take notes in your notebook about what they say and add them to your chart.

5. Discuss the questions with the class.

1. Which natural disaster does the class know most about?

2. Which was the most recent?

In this unit, you will practice inferring the meaning from a lecture or text.

Previewing the Academic Skills Focus

Inference

Sometimes people don't state what they mean directly. They indirectly say, or imply, what they mean. As a reader or listener, you have to **infer** their meaning from other clues.

To try to understand implied meaning, pay attention to:

- Intonation: the rise and fall of the person's voice.
- Context: what people are saying and doing at that time, and other information given.
- Logic: connecting related information.

Think like a detective. Use any clues you can find.

1. 🎧 *Listen to two earth science professors talking. Complete the chart.*

Point	True or False	Clue
One professor is angry at the government.	*true*	*intonation; context*
The government is very active in dealing with this problem.		
Cotton farming uses a lot of water.		
Rice farming uses a lot of water.		
A mistake was made in the past.		
It's easy for farmers to change what they grow.		

2. *How did you know what to answer? Circle the correct answer.*

    a. things the professors said directly
    b. things the professors said indirectly that I inferred

Large-scale irrigation on cotton fields in California

2

Building Academic Reading Skills

In this section, you will practice making inferences from the context of what you are reading. You will also learn about drawing conclusions.

For online assignments, go to

Before You Read

Work with a partner. Look at the pictures. Guess the answers to the questions.

Fishing boat left behind by the sea

Villagers gathering salt from what was once the sea

1. What do you think has happened?
2. Why do you think it happened?
3. What do you think the results will be for the local people?

Global Reading

1. Skim the excerpt from an environmental science textbook.

Key Words

dramatically *adv* very large and surprisingly; **drama** *n*; **dramatic** *adj*

extinct *adj* no longer existing; **extinction** *n*

impact *v* to have an effect on something— often the effect is a problem; **impact** *n*

THE SHRINKING of the ARAL SEA

1   In the former Soviet Union, one of the world's worst environmental disasters took place: The death of the Aral Sea. The Aral Sea is in Kazakhstan and Uzbekistan. In the 1930s, the government decided to grow cotton there. The cotton would earn money as an export. But cotton needs lots of water. The only way to supply the water was through irrigation. So, water was taken from the Amu Darya and the Syr Darya, the two large rivers flowing into the Aral. By 1960, these rivers supplied water to a very large area of farm land. The Soviet Union became the world's second-largest cotton exporter, and the project appeared to be a great success.

2   However, the amount of water flowing into the sea became much smaller. From the 12 cubic[1] miles (50 cubic kilometers) the sea received in 1965, it fell to zero by the early 1980s (and the 1965 amount was already much

---

[1] **cubic** *n* a unit for measuring volume; calculated by multiplying the length of something by its width and height

(continued on next page)

Aral Sea

5   Farming in the countries around the sea, Uzbekistan and Kazakhstan, still depends on irrigation from the rivers feeding the sea. Turkmenistan, Tajikistan, and Kyrgyzstan also take water from the Amu Darya and the Syr Darya for irrigation. These five countries all have economic problems, and the diverted waters support billions of dollars' worth of farming every year, supporting millions of workers. It is unlikely, therefore, that those countries will agree to take less water from the rivers. In any event, it will be very difficult to restore the sea to its original size. It would take 50 years of no irrigation just to double the sea's area, and the process would destroy the nearby economies.

6   The Aral Sea is breaking up into several smaller lakes. In one or two of these, fishing may be possible in the future if the rivers are allowed to fill them directly. The key is to let more water flow in and thus stop the increase in the salinity of the area. By making the irrigation systems more efficient, this is possible. The countries have little money to spend, however, so they must rely on international organizations for help. The World Bank has lent $64 million to Kazakhstan to help the northern Aral Sea so that fishing can start again.

less than in the 1930s). Not surprisingly, the sea, once 26,000 square miles (68,000 square kilometers) in area, began to shrink.

3   The earliest impact was to the large fishing industry. There were 60,000 people who had worked in this industry. Because basically no new water was entering the sea, the salinity began to increase as water evaporated. This destroyed life in the sea. The sea is now three times as salty as the ocean. The fishing industry collapsed by the early 1980s. The sea lost 80 percent of its original volume and the water level dropped more than 56 feet (17 meters).

4   There are other impacts as well. The now-dry sea bed contains salts. The dry winds of the area pick up the salt and dust and drop them on the irrigated land, causing breathing problems for people for miles around and carrying the pollution as far as the Arctic and Pakistan. Many health impacts have affected the area, including cancer and higher infant mortality.[2] The local climate has changed: The season for growing food has become shorter. This has forced many farmers to change from cotton to other crops. Many animal species unique to the Aral Sea have become extinct.

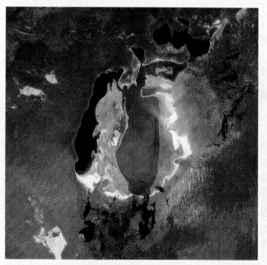

Aral Sea viewed from space

---

[2] **higher infant mortality** *n* more deaths of children

Source: Adapted from Wright, R. (2005). *Environmental science: Toward a sustainable future* (9th ed.). Upper Saddle River, NJ: Pearson Prentice Hall.

2. Read the flyer from an environmental organization. Complete the sentences with information from the reading on pages 131–132.

WHERE DID OUR SEA GO?

One of the worst environmental disasters in human history involves a whole sea nearly disappearing.

The Aral Sea used to be in the Soviet Union but is now shared between Uzbekistan and Kazakhstan. The problem was caused by (1) _____. As a result, (2) _____ fell dramatically. Consequently, the volume of water in the sea fell by 80 percent between 1960 and the early 1980s.

The first main impact involved (3) _____. Later impacts included (4) _____, people's health, local climate change, and extinction of species.

Uzbekistan and Kazakhstan now have (5) _____ but still need (6) _____. There may be hope for some sections of the sea, though. The sea is (7) _____.

If more water can flow into these, some areas may return to something similar to their previous state. For that to happen, though, more money is needed, and that can only come from the international community.

Focused Reading

Inferring Meaning from Context

Inference can be very useful for your language learning. When you find words you don't know, you can often infer something about their meaning from the context—the other words around them.

For example, the text said, "The only way to supply the water was through irrigation." Even if you don't know the word *irrigation*, you can see that it is about supplying water. Then the text said that the water went to farm land. So, you can infer that *irrigation* means *supplying water to farm land.*

You might not find the exact meaning using this skill, but often it is close enough.

climate *n*

crops *n*

efficient *adj*

evaporated *v*

irrigation *n*

salinity *n*

shrink *v*

volume *n*

1. *Read the text again carefully. Infer the meaning of the key words from the context of the reading. Write each word next to its definition.*

1. _____ working well, quickly, and without wasting time, energy, or effort (paragraph 6)

2. _____ changed into a gas (not steam) due to heat such as the sun's heat (paragraph 3)

3. _____ to get smaller (paragraph 2)

4. _____ types of plant that farmers grow for food (paragraph 4)

5. _____ supplying water to farm land (paragraph 1)

6. _____ amount of salt (paragraph 3)

7. _____ the amount of something, measured in gallons, cubic miles, etc. (paragraph 3)

8. _____ the typical weather in an area (paragraph 4)

2. *Work with a partner. Make inferences about whether the author is likely to agree with the statements. Write **L** (likely) or **U** (unlikely). What evidence is there? Discuss how you chose your answers. Then work with another pair. Compare and discuss answers.*

_____ 1. Cotton growing was very successful at first. (paragraphs 1 and 2)

_____ 2. The lifestyle of the people around the Aral Sea has suffered over the last 40 years. (paragraphs 3 and 4)

_____ 3. Not looking after the environment can affect unexpected things, such as people's health. (paragraph 4)

_____ 4. The Aral Sea is now the responsibility only of Kazakhstan and Uzbekistan. (paragraph 5)

_____ 5. People should look at the long-term effects as well as short-term benefits of a project. (the whole text)

Sugarloaf Reservoir near Melbourne, Australia. This reservoir has shrunk to 27% of its normal volume.

In your academic studies, you will have to draw conclusions. **Drawing a conclusion** means looking at all the information you have about a topic and making a guess or forming an opinion about that information. Your conclusion is an inference based on the information you have.

By drawing conclusions, you can show that you understand ideas and form opinions based on these ideas.

To draw conclusions:

- Look at all the information you can find. Look for connections and patterns in this information. Try to think of consequences, ideas for future actions, or solutions to problems. These are your conclusions.
- Check again that your conclusions fit the facts. Remember that a conclusion is usually a guess or an opinion that is based on information given.

3. *Work with a partner. Based on information in the reading, what conclusions can you draw? Think about future actions, consequences, and possible solutions to problems.*

1. The governments of Kazakhstan and Uzbekistan should *take action* _____ *quickly. They need to repair the damage to the Aral Sea. They need to find something to replace the cotton industry—something that needs less water. They also should* _____

    _____

2. The governments of other, wealthier, countries should _____

    _____

    _____

    _____

3. People living in the area should _____

    _____

    _____

    _____

4. Farmers and people responsible for irrigation projects should _____

    _____

    _____

    _____

Checkpoint 1   PEARSON LONGMAN   myacademicconnectionslab

 Unit 8 ■ The Water Cycle   **135**

3
Building Academic Listening Skills

In this section, you will practice inferring a speaker's purpose or intention.

For online assignments, go to

PEARSON LONGMAN
myacademicconnectionslab

Key Words

filter (through) *v* to pass through something that stops unwanted pieces from getting past; **filter** *n*

ground *n* the surface of the land

groundwater *n* water within the earth especially that supplies wells and springs

precipitation *n* rain or snow; any form of water falling from the sky

reservoir *n* a large area where water is stored

sediment *n* sand, stone, mud, etc. that falls to the bottom of rivers and lakes

soak (through) *v* to pass through something, making it wet

spring *n* a place where water comes to the surface naturally

stream *n* a small river

Before You Listen

The diagram shows how the water cycle (hydrologic cycle) works naturally, without humans doing anything to it. Work with a partner. Write the key words in their correct places on the lines.

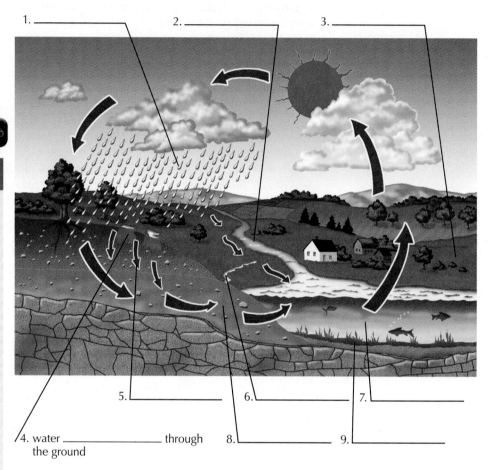

1. _____ 2. _____ 3. _____

4. water _____ through the ground 5. _____ 6. _____ 7. _____ 8. _____ 9. _____

Figure 8.1 Hydrologic cycle

Global Listening

1. 🎧 *Listen to the lecture. Number the topics in the order you hear them. One of the ideas is mentioned but is not a main idea. Which one is it?*

___1___ the natural water cycle   _____ springs, streams, and rivers

_____ Bangladesh, as an example   _____ changes to the water cycle

_____ floods

2. *What is the professor's attitude toward the effect of humans on the water cycle—positive, neutral, or negative? How do you know?*

Focused Listening

1. 🎧 *Listen to an excerpt from the lecture. As you listen to the description of a natural water cycle, check off (✓) the arrows on the diagram on page 136.*

2. 🎧 *Listen to another excerpt from the lecture. As you listen to the description of what happens when humans interfere in the water cycle, cross out the arrows that show the flow that decreases, and circle the arrows showing the flow that increases.*

3. 🎧 *Work with a partner. Look at the cause-effect diagram. Predict where the words and expressions from the box fit in the digram. Then listen to check and complete your answers.*

~~cutting down trees~~	filtration stops; water runs directly to waterways	more sediment and pollution
~~erosion~~	floods	overuse of land

CAUSES   **CHAIN OF EFFECTS**

- *cutting down trees* _____
  _____
- _____
  _____

→

- _____
  _____
  _____
  _____

→

- _____
- *erosion* _____

↓

- _____
  _____
  _____
  _____

4. 🎧 *Work with the same partner. Look at the cause-effect diagram on page 138. Predict where the expresions from the box fit in the diagram. Then listen to check and complete your answers.*

bottom of river rises	more erosion	~~more floods~~	more sediment
less filtering of water	more farming	more tree cutting	~~worse floods~~

(continued on next page)

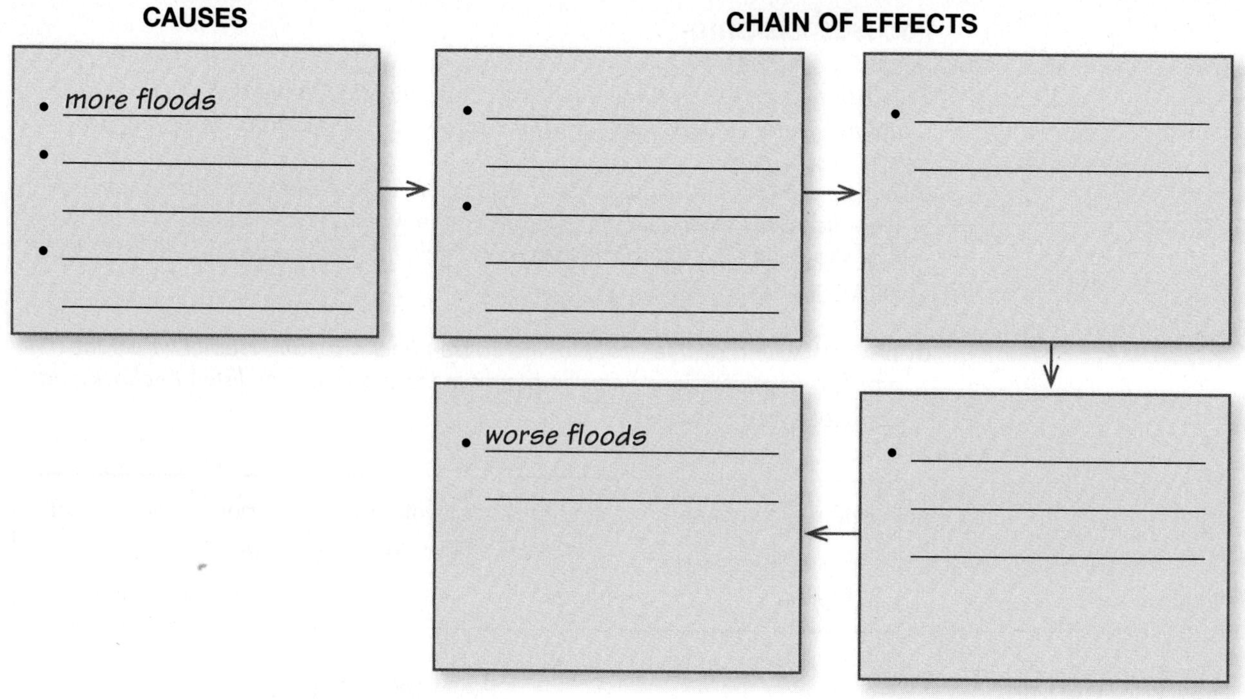

CAUSES

- _more floods_
- _____
  _____
- _____
  _____

CHAIN OF EFFECTS

- _____
  _____
- _____
  _____

- _____
  _____

- _worse floods_
  _____

- _____
  _____
  _____

5. 🎧 *Work with the same partner. Look at the cause-effect diagram. Predict where the expressions from the box fit in the diagram. Then listen to check and complete your answers.*

groundwater reservoirs have less water	less water can evaporate	~~springs dry up~~
less rainfall	problems for people	streams dry up

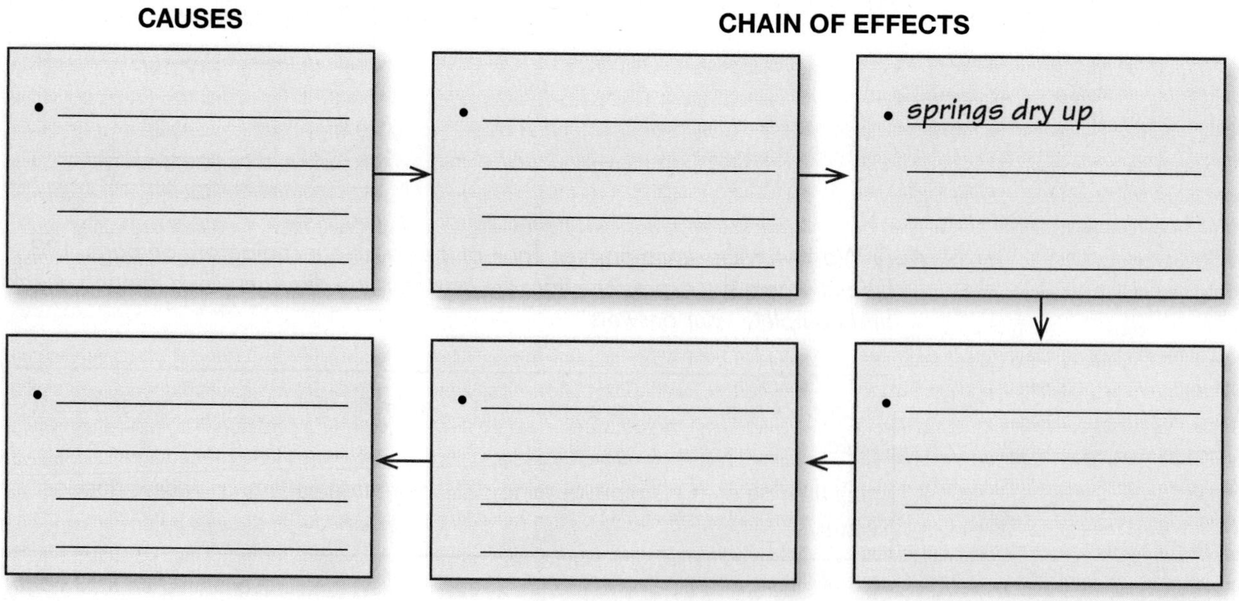

CAUSES

- _____
  _____
  _____

- _____
  _____
  _____

CHAIN OF EFFECTS

- _____
  _____
  _____

- _springs dry up_
  _____
  _____

- _____
  _____
  _____

- _____
  _____
  _____

You looked at the speaker's purpose in Unit 7. You also saw how a speaker can have more than one purpose. Now you can also use inference to help find the speaker's purpose.

To do this, ask yourself these questions:

- What possible purposes did the speaker have?
- Which purposes best fit the situation?

6. *Listen to the excerpts from the lecture. Check (✓) the correct purpose. There may be more than one correct answer.*

⌒ Excerpt One

❏ To show unhappiness
❏ To encourage students to study hard

⌒ Excerpt Two

❏ To give homework
❏ To show what is important for the test

⌒ Excerpt Three

❏ To explain an important process
❏ To give the scope of the lecture

⌒ Excerpt Four

❏ To link current ideas to past knowledge
❏ To remind students about something from an earlier lecture

⌒ Excerpt Five

❏ To tell students to look in their books
❏ To show students what they can look at later if they didn't understand something

7. *Write a paragraph in your notebook to answer the questions. Complete the chart on the next page to help you prepare. When you write your paragraph, give the conclusion you draw in the topic sentence.*

- What are two ways that humans have affected the water cycle?
- What effects have these had?
- What conclusion can you draw from these facts?

(continued on next page)

	From the Reading	From the Lecture
The main ways that humans affected the water cycle		
Effects of these interventions		
A conclusion you can draw from the point you've chosen		

4

Building Academic Speaking Skills

In this section, you will practice using intonation to convey meaning and persuade your audience. Then you will speak about problems caused by human intervention in the water cycle using information from the reading, the lecture, and a podcast.

For online assignments, go to

Before You Speak

1. 🎧 *Listen to a podcast from an environmental organization. How strongly do you think the speaker feels about the issue?*

Glacier

2. 🎧 *Listen again to the podcast and complete the summary by filling in the missing words. Compare your answers with a partner's.*

Glaciers in the Himalayas are (1) _____. This is causing

(2) _____ to flow into several major rivers, such as

the Mekong, Yangtze, Indus, and Ganges. In the short term, this will

cause (3) _____. In the long term, after the glaciers

(4) _____, there will be less water for (5) _____.

The number of people that could be affected is (6) _____.

3. 🎧 *Listen to the sentences from the podcast. Do they go down or up at the end? Circle the correct answer for each sentence.*

1. a. ↗ b. ↘   3. a. ↗ b. ↘
2. a. ↗ b. ↘   4. a. ↗ b. ↘

4. *Do you think the speaker is sure of what he is saying? Explain.*

Using Intonation to Convey Meaning

Falling intonation at the end of a clause shows that the speaker is sure of his or her facts. Use falling intonation to show that you are sure about something.

Rising intonation at the end of a clause shows the speaker is unsure and wants some information. That is why questions usually have rising intonation at the end.

5. *In your notebook, write three statements and three questions related to the reading, lecture, or podcast in this unit. Then work with a partner. Take turns. One student says a sentence or question from the list, using either rising or falling intonation. The other student points to the scale to show how sure the speaker seems to be.*

←――――――――――――――――――――――――――――――――――→

NOT SURE   SURE

Focused Speaking

1. 🎧 *Listen to the podcast again. Which do you think best describes the purpose of the podcast? Circle the correct answer.*

 a. to persuade people that the problem exists
 b. to give information
 c. to show how much the speaker knows
 d. to scare people

2. 🎧 *Listen to the last sentence of the podcast. Why do you think the speaker paused?*

Persuading Your Audience

Often, speakers have to persuade their audience, such as a professor or other students, that an opinion is correct. This is common in presentations.

The best way to do this is to provide strong evidence. In addition, you can:

 • Use stress and intonation to sound enthusiastic about your opinion.
 • Use falling intonation to sound certain about your ideas and information.
 • Use dramatic pauses where appropriate.

Be careful! If you use these three techniques without showing good evidence, people might not trust you. The most important thing is good evidence.

3. *Work with a partner. Choose one of the statements. Then list as much evidence as you can from the reading, listening, and podcast to support your statement.*

- Human intervention in the water cycle causes seas to dry up.
- Human intervention in the water cycle causes floods.
- Human intervention in the water cycle may cause food supply problems.

4. *Work alone to prepare a short speech (about one minute long) to persuade someone that your statement is correct. It should include:*

- Strong supporting ideas.
- Intonation showing that you believe what you're saying and that you're enthusiastic about it.
- Dramatic pauses.

5. *Work with a new partner. Listen to each other's speeches. As you listen, complete the chart. Write **Yes** or **No** in each category. Give your partner feedback and explain. After you get feedback on your speech, work with another partner, and repeat the process. Did you get better as you practiced? Explain.*

Name	Used Strong Supporting Ideas	Intonation Made Statements Sound Truthful	Sounded Enthusiastic	Used Dramatic Pauses
Yuki	Yes	No	Yes	No

Integrated Speaking Task

You have read a text and listened to a lecture and podcast about the hydrologic cycle. You will now use your knowledge of the content, vocabulary, intonation, and persuasion to give a persuasive talk in response to this question: **What problems are caused by human intervention in the water cycle?**

Follow the steps to prepare your talk.

Step 1: Divide the class into three groups: A, B, and C.

        Group A: Look again at the main reading for this unit.

        Group B: Listen to the lecture again.

        Group C: Listen to the podcast again.

Step 2: Work with another person from your group. Look at the chart. Add causes of the problems listed. Then add other problems that you read or heard about and their causes.

Problem	Cause	Solution
Waterways dry up		
Floods		
Food supply problems		

Step 3: Form new groups of three. Each group should have a person from group A, B, and C. Tell your new group what you found and add their ideas to the chart. Then think of some possible solutions to the problems. Make notes of your ideas in the right-hand column of the chart.

Step 4: Choose one (or two) problems. Prepare your talk. You may want to use this format for your talk:

    Part 1: how humans interfere

    Part 2: what effect it has

    Part 3: what we can do / why we should stop interfering

Step 5: Practice your talk in your groups.

Step 6: Form new groups of three, but make sure no one from your previous group is in this group. Give your talks. While you listen to the other student's talks, complete the chart.

Student's Name	Main Idea	Supporting Ideas	Persuasive Techniques Used
1.			
2.			
3.			

Step 7: Vote on who in your group is the most persuasive and discuss why.

AUDIOSCRIPT

UNIT 1

Biology: Experiments and the Common Cold

Global Listening

Exercise 2, Page 11

Professor: Good morning all, glad to see you're all here on time—wonderful. This morning, we're going to continue to discuss research methods, which is what we were talking about last week. Anyone remember the name of the method we said we'd talk about this week?

Student: The experimental method?

Professor: Yep, that's it. Today, we'll look at the experimental method in more detail, and some of the more important points we'll discuss are controls and controlled experiments, placebos, blind experiments, and double-blind experiments. As we'll see, most experiments, in biology are in fact controlled experiments, and placebos are very useful for making sure that controlled experiments are also blind experiments. These ideas are all very, very important things to think about every time you hear about an experiment.

Lecture: The Experimental Method

Professor: Good morning all, glad to see you're all here on time—wonderful. This morning, we're going to continue to discuss research methods, which is what we were talking about last week. Anyone remember the name of the method we said we'd talk about this week?

Student: The experimental method?

Professor: Yep, that's it. Today, we'll look at the experimental method in more detail, and some of the more important points we'll discuss are controls and controlled experiments, placebos, blind experiments, and double-blind experiments. As we'll see, most experiments, in biology are in fact controlled experiments, and placebos are very useful for making sure that controlled experiments are also blind experiments. These ideas are all very, very important things to think about every time you hear about an experiment.

First of all, controlled experiments. The best way to explain these is with an example, which we'll look at over the next few minutes. Maybe some of you drink echinacea tea when you have a cold, yes? No? OK, for those of you who don't know about echinacea tea, it's a kind of herbal tea made from parts of the echinacea flower. But do you know whether it's effective? Of course you see lots of advertisements saying it is—they wouldn't sell much if they didn't, would they! So, how can we be sure?

Our example experiment will help us find out. For instance, scientists could give echinacea tea to a group of people and see whether their colds got better more quickly than "normal." This group is the experimental group. But what's "normal"? The experiment needs another group of people who don't get any echinacea tea. Then, if there's a difference between the two groups, maybe, just maybe, this difference is from taking echinacea. So, the control group is the same as the experimental group, but does not get the experimental treatment. Or in other words, the only difference between the experimental group and the control is the reason for the experiment, the treatment. In this case, the treatment is the echinacea tea.

But the people, the participants, shouldn't know which group they're in. If they know they're taking the real treatment or medicine, this by itself may make them feel positive and thus, feel better. Likewise, if people know they're in the control group, they may feel they're not getting better because they know they're not taking any medicine. Just knowing which group you're in can make a real difference—people who think they are getting the actual treatment sometimes feel better just because of their thinking.

But, you're probably wondering, how can people not know which group they're in? Surely, they know when they're not taking the treatment! Scientists have an answer for that—and it's an important answer—they give something called a placebo. The spelling is—I'll write it on the board—p-l-a-c-e-b-o. What is a placebo? It's something that does nothing. It has no effect. But it looks just like the medicine, the treatment. In our echinacea experiment, for example, the placebo looks just like the echinacea tea.

This leads us to our next idea. When participants don't know which group they're in, we say they are blinded. They can't see whether they are taking the real treatment or the placebo.

This brings us to the next point. Sometimes, the research assistants—the people giving the treatment (in our case, the echinacea tea)—are also "blinded." That is, they don't know whether they are giving real tea or not. This is just in case they accidentally give hints about whether it's real tea.

When the research assistants and the participants are all blinded, we call it a "double-blind" experiment. OK, I think that's enough for today…

Focused Writing

Exercise 4, Page 17

Radio announcer: Well, it's an amazing world, isn't it? Just when you think you know something, scientists come along and tell you it's wrong. Did you know that some biologists announced recently that vitamin C has no effect on catching a cold? No effect! Unbelievable! After what we've been told for so many years!

So, how do the scientists know? Well, apparently they found a very large number of volunteers. They gave extra vitamin C to half of the volunteers but not the other half. All the volunteers kept a diary for a year, of all their colds and cold symptoms, and at the end of the year the scientists counted how many colds each group had. And both groups had almost the same—in fact, the group taking vitamin C actually got a few more colds! So now we know, vitamin C seems to have no effect. However, the scientists did say that if you already have a cold, vitamin C can help you get better sooner. And of course vitamin C is good for you in general anyway.

And what about staying warm—wrapping up in a blanket or a warm sweater—just like people told you to do when you were a kid? That doesn't work, either. There is apparently no connection between low temperatures and getting colds.

So, what do scientists now say you should do to prevent colds? Well, just wash your hands. That's all—simple! Scientists say that the cold virus can live on surfaces for several hours—wash your hands, and the viruses are gone. So, there you have it. Good ole' soap and water works wonders! On that note, here's a rainy day message…

UNIT 2

Marketing: New Ways to Spread the Message

Global Listening

Exercise 1, Page 26

Professor: Good morning, everyone. Good morning. Let's start off today with one of the recent trends in advertising. As we said last week, we see so many ads in our daily lives that many people now just don't even notice them, do they? Many people just stop looking when they see an ad. Consequently, companies aren't getting their message across. Also, normal advertisements such as those on TV, in magazines, and on the Internet are getting expensive.

Therefore, companies need to find lower-cost strategies to make people notice their products. Today, we'll look at some new marketing strategies to help to solve these problems. First, we'll look at viral marketing, and then, stealth marketing.

Exercise 2, Page 26

Professor: So, first of all, viral marketing. The name sounds bad, doesn't it? Viral marketing… Actually, when marketing people say *viral*, they don't mean catching a cold or some other illness. What they really mean is that the advertising message spreads very naturally and quickly from one person to another all by itself. This is similar to how a cold spreads, or a computer virus. Basically, in viral marketing, the company thinks of a cool, interesting message—it has to be interesting so that people will want to tell it to their friends straight away. In this way, the people become the advertising medium. This is much cheaper than expensive TV time slots or space in a magazine. Here's an example. Google, when they first marketed gmail™, their e-mail service, made it invitation only. Anyone who got an invitation could give away more invitations to their friends. That was clever. The clever bit was to control the number of invitations, so that people felt special when they got one—but not so many that everyone had one.

There are two main advantages to viral marketing. First, it works by word of mouth. This is highly effective because people usually believe their friends more than they believe advertisements. It's true. Secondly, as you've probably guessed—it's cheap, because of course there are none of the high costs of normal advertising.

The next type of marketing to talk about is stealth marketing. Actually, this is really a type of viral marketing. The main difference here is that in stealth marketing, unlike viral marketing, no one knows that it's advertising—aha! Because it doesn't look like advertising. Let's have an example. At least one stealth marketer in the U.S., a movie company, gave T-shirts and posters to teenagers as young as 13. In exchange, the teenagers agreed to talk to their friends at school and on Internet chat sites about the movies that the company was marketing. Clever, isn't it? But the company also told them to keep quiet about who they are working for. Sounds great for the company, doesn't it? Because just like viral marketing, it's cheap and works very effectively through word of mouth. However, you can probably see the danger area here. If the parents find out, they will feel that the company is tricking and using their children. This could make people really dislike the brand… really have a bad opinion of it. So, just like viral marketing, stealth marketing is cheap and can be extremely effective— but it is also a dangerous game to play.

Exercise 3, Page 26

Professor: So there we have it—viral marketing and stealth marketing. Many companies are very excited about these, especially companies selling to younger people. It's early days yet—these strategies haven't been around for very long—but it would be very interesting to see what happens over the next few years. Will viral and stealth marketing become standard, normal strategies that many companies will choose? Or is it just a fashion that no one will remember in a few years? We'll just have to wait and see.

Lecture: New Ways in Advertising

Professor: Good morning, everyone. Good morning. Let's start off today with one of the recent trends in advertising. As we said last week, we see so many ads in our daily lives that many people now just don't even notice them, do they? Many people just stop looking when they see an ad. Consequently, companies aren't getting their message across. Also, normal advertisements such as those on TV, in magazines, and on the Internet are getting expensive. Therefore, companies need to find lower-cost strategies to make people notice their products. Today, we'll look at some new marketing strategies to help to solve these problems. First, we'll look at viral marketing, and then, stealth marketing.

So, first of all, viral marketing. The name sounds bad, doesn't it? Viral marketing… Actually, when marketing people say *viral*, they don't mean catching a cold or some other illness. What they really mean is that the advertising message spreads very naturally and quickly from one person to another all by itself. This is similar to how a cold spreads, or a computer virus. Basically, in viral marketing, the company thinks of a cool, interesting message—it has to be interesting so that people will want to tell it to their friends straight away. In this way, the people become the advertising medium. This is much cheaper than expensive TV time slots or space in a magazine. Here's an example. Google, when they first marketed gmail™, their e-mail service, made it invitation only. Anyone who got an invitation could give away more invitations to their friends. That was clever. The clever bit was to control the number of invitations, so that people felt special when they got one—but not so many that everyone had one.

There are two main advantages to viral marketing. First, it works by word of mouth. This is highly effective because people usually believe their friends more than they believe advertisements. It's true. Secondly, as you've probably guessed—it's cheap, because of course there are none of the high costs of normal advertising.

The next type of marketing to talk about is stealth marketing. Actually, this is really a type of viral marketing. The main difference here is that in stealth marketing, unlike viral marketing, no one knows that it's advertising—aha! Because it doesn't look like advertising. Let's have an example. At least one stealth marketer in the U.S., a movie company, gave T-shirts and posters to teenagers as young as 13. In exchange, the teenagers agreed to talk to their friends at school and on Internet chat sites about the movies that the company was marketing. Clever, isn't it? But the company also told them to keep quiet about who they are working for. Sounds great for the company, doesn't it? Because just like viral marketing, it's cheap and works very effectively through word of mouth. However, you can probably see the danger area here. If the parents find out, they will feel that the company is tricking and using their children. This could make people really dislike the brand… really have a bad opinion of it. So, just like viral marketing, stealth marketing is cheap and can be extremely effective—but it is also a dangerous game to play.

So there we have it—viral marketing and stealth marketing. Many companies are very excited about these, especially companies selling to younger people. It's early days yet—these strategies haven't been around for very long—but it would be very interesting to see what happens over the next few years. Will viral and stealth marketing become standard, normal strategies that many companies will choose? Or is it just a fashion that no one will remember in a few years? We'll just have to wait and see.

Before You Speak

Page 35

Professor: OK. I'll give you some suggestions for your project. As we mentioned before, the key to viral and stealth marketing is the message. There are two important points about that. First, it *must* be interesting, so that people really *want* to tell their friends, right? That isn't actually too difficult if the product really is interesting. Second, there must be an easy way for people to get the message. OK, here are some strategies that have worked in the past. One is to have a reason to talk to other people, strangers I mean. For example, you might pretend to be a tourist, and ask someone to take your picture. Then, you can start a conversation about where you've been that day, or even about your camera or maybe your cell phone. Another idea is to put stickers on lamp posts or other similar places, with some mysterious information. That could be some surprising news, or an interesting website. Anything that makes people want to look it up on their cell phone.

UNIT 3

Astronomy: Collisions from Space

Lecture: Are Asteroids and Comets Dangerous?

Professor: Good morning! Well, I hope it's a good morning!

So, where are we? … Oh, yes, we saw in the last lecture that an asteroid collision could've killed the dinosaurs. But could this event happen again? I mean, could a meteorite hit Earth and kill off the main life forms? You may have seen bad films such as *Deep Impact* or *Armageddon* … but is there any reality to them?

Well, the scary answer seems to be: Yes, this could happen! Asteroids and comets are very common in the solar system. To see evidence of this, just look at the Moon. It's covered in craters! And what caused these? Well, it's pretty clear that it was asteroids and comets—nothing else could do that.

So, why isn't Earth covered in craters, just like the Moon and some of the planets? Well, there are two reasons. For one thing, Earth has an atmosphere but the Moon doesn't. Earth's atmosphere slows asteroids down, causing heat which burns off their outer layers. Again, you can see this process yourself. Have you ever seen shooting stars? They are actually the remains of broken up comets. It is the burning that we can see. Most are very small, so they burn up completely and disappear before they get close to the ground.

Another reason comes from geology. Earth's surface is constantly moving—as you probably know, this is called the plate tectonic theory, and is the reason for earthquakes. When plates collide with each other, Earth's surface gets pushed up. In this way, mountains or islands are formed. When the continents move apart, huge valleys and seas are created. Thus, a map of Earth from the dinosaur's time would've looked very, very different from now. You can easily see how craters disappear as the land changes shape.

It's clear, therefore, that the lack of craters doesn't mean we're safe! Scientists predict that a large asteroid, as big as the one that probably killed the dinosaurs, should hit Earth, on average, once every 10 million years. But it's 65 million years since the last one! Smaller asteroids are passing close to Earth all the time. Only in 1989, an asteroid around 1,000 feet in diameter—that's about 300 meters—called 4581 Asclepius, passed through the point where Earth was just six hours before. A hit from it would have caused the largest explosion in history. On average, researchers say, an object big enough to cause catastrophic results, will hit Earth every 5000 years.

So, we know so far that there's a high chance of meteorites hitting Earth some time in the future. The next important question is what can we—or rather, the governments we vote for—do about it? Well, firstly, they need to find out if there are any asteroids or comets heading for Earth.

Astronomers are already working on this. Since the late 1990s, NASA has been conducting several surveys of space, the biggest of which is LINEAR. NASA aims to find 90 percent of all the near-Earth objects, in other words, NEOs, that are more than two thirds of a mile—one kilometer—in diameter. So far, tens of thousands of them have been found—most of them, fortunately, too far away to be dangerous for now. Also, a couple of near-misses have been identified, although usually rather late—after the object has passed Earth. In 2002, an object 250 feet—about 80 meters—in diameter passed only 75,000 miles—that's about 120,000 kilometers—from Earth. A hit from that would have caused as much destruction as a nuclear weapon. Current estimates suggest that an object large enough to destroy a city passes closer than the Moon every month. As technology improves, we will get better information about these objects.

But, if we find one heading straight towards Earth, the harder question is what to do then? Destroying the asteroid won't work. A nuclear weapon could smash it into many pieces quite easily. But that would just mean many objects hitting Earth instead of one. Probably a better way is to find out how to change the asteroid's direction … but a project like that would cost trillions of dollars, and at the moment it doesn't seem that governments are willing to pay for such research.

The chances are that, if we do find a very dangerous object coming straight towards us, we'll have several years to work out what to do. Perhaps if we do find a danger, that will motivate governments to spend the necessary money … and perhaps even work together to do so.

UNIT 4

Acting: Imagination

Lecture: Using Your Imagination on Stage

Professor: Good afternoon, everyone. How are you all? Well, as promised today, we have our guest lecturer, Gene Blake, who's going to tell us a little about his experiences as an actor. As you know, Mr. Blake has appeared in more than 30 films, has had a long career on the stage, and now teaches master classes at acting schools all around the world. Today, I've asked him to focus on how he has used imagination to achieve success. But first, let's just remind ourselves how we define imagination. As we saw last time, to an actor, imagination is any process in which we think about anything that we are not currently experiencing. This can be in preparation for a role, and it can also be during the performance. It is a way of putting ourselves in the mind of the character. It can be based on personal experience, of similar emotions and situations to our character, for example. Or it can be based on research. Or, more likely, a combination of these. So, please welcome Mr. Gene Blake.

Gene Blake: Yes, thank you, Professor Whitely, and thank you to everyone for having me here today. Well, I'll get straight into it. Imagination, I believe, is one of the most important things for an actor. Imagination can help you to play your role realistically. Think about this. Your character may live a life that is very different from your own. You will thus need imagination to understand your character's reactions and feelings. And it's really, really important to understand your character's feelings. This is absolutely necessary for making your character look real and genuine to the audience—in other words, necessary for giving an authentic performance.

So, when I'm asked to play a new character, where do I start? The first step, clearly, is to prepare for the role by researching it. To be sure of an authentic performance, you have to be sure that your starting point is truthful. If you're playing a historical role, make sure you understand the period of history. If you're playing someone from a very different sector of society, make sure you understand the lifestyles and everyday activities of those people. And, to my mind, research for actors does not just mean reading— you need to spend time with people like your characters, spend time living like them. Give your imagination the best possible starting point.

I'll give you an example of this. Years ago, I played the role of a person who was completely disabled—my character couldn't move any part of his body at all, except his head. Now, I can't make myself disabled—that would be a terrible thing to do, wouldn't it? But I did spend a lot of time with disabled people before filming started. I also tried to live the life of a disabled person. I continued doing it during filming as well, to keep my mind as focused as possible on the mind of the character. For example, I tied myself to a wheelchair, and insisted that people carry me up steps when really I could easily walk up them myself, that kind of thing. This drove people crazy, but I remember that it helped, helped a lot. I remember one person who just hated having to lift me up the steps to the dressing room. I remember he got quite angry.

Of course, the key to making all this work is imagination. Just going through the motions isn't enough. You just can't fit into a few months the whole lifetime of experiences that your character would have had. With the disabled character, there was a lifetime of frustration and of dealing with people's reactions to the disability—experiences I just didn't have. So, to fill this gap, I had to use imagination. Even though my character was an adult, I spent a lot of time thinking through, imagining, how common childhood

experiences would be different because of the disability; how that would have an emotional effect on the adult me. Because of course, people are shaped by their experiences. And this hard work paid off—I won an award for the role. What a celebration we had after that! We were partying for days!

But of course, personal experiences can be very, very useful for some roles. I played a London gang member once. Now, I'm not British, as you know, but I did have some experiences in my younger days with, shall we say, some of the less friendly people in New York. Some of these experiences helped me to understand what it feels like to be living on the edges of society. It wasn't exactly the same, of course, and you'll never have exactly the same life experiences as your character. But, imagination is a way to fill that gap, too.

So, those are my thoughts. Any questions?

Student: Yes, Mr. Blake. I was wondering… on your first film…

Focused Listening
Exercise 1, Page 59

Professor: Good afternoon, everyone. How are you all? Well, as promised today, we have our guest lecturer, Gene Blake, who's going to tell us a little about his experiences as an actor. As you know, Mr. Blake has appeared in more than 30 films, has had a long career on the stage, and now teaches master classes at acting schools all around the world. Today, I've asked him to focus on how he has used imagination to achieve success. But first, let's just remind ourselves how we define imagination. As we saw last time, to an actor, imagination is any process in which we think about anything that we are not currently experiencing. This can be in preparation for a role, and it can also be during the performance. It is a way of putting ourselves in the mind of the character. It can be based on personal experience, of similar emotions and situations to our character, for example. Or it can be based on research. Or, more likely, a combination of these. So, please welcome Mr. Gene Blake.

Exercise 3, Page 60

Gene Blake: Yes, thank you, Professor Whitely, and thank you to everyone for having me here today. Well, I'll get straight into it. Imagination, I believe, is one of the most important things for an actor. Imagination can help you to play your role realistically. Think about this. Your character may live a life that is very different from your own. You will thus need imagination to understand your character's reactions and feelings. And it's really, really important to understand your character's feelings. This is absolutely necessary for making your character look real and genuine to the audience—in other words, necessary for giving an authentic performance.

So, when I'm asked to play a new character, where do I start? The first step, clearly, is to prepare for the role by researching it. To be sure of an authentic performance, you have to be sure that your starting point is truthful. If you're playing a historical role, make sure you understand the period of history. If you're playing someone from a very different sector of society, make sure you understand the lifestyles and everyday activities of those people. And, to my mind, research for actors does not just mean reading—you need to spend time with people like your characters, spend time living like them. Give your imagination the best possible starting point.

I'll give you an example of this. Years ago, I played the role of a person who was completely disabled—my character couldn't move any part of his body at all, except his head. Now, I can't make myself disabled—that would be a terrible thing to do, wouldn't it? But I did spend a lot of time with disabled people before filming started. I also tried to live the life of a disabled person. I continued doing it during filming as well, to keep my mind as focused as possible on the mind of the character. For example, I tied myself to a wheelchair, and insisted that people carry me up steps when really I could easily walk up them myself, that kind of thing. This drove people crazy, but I remember that it helped, helped a lot. I remember one person who just hated having to lift me up the steps to the dressing room. I remember he got quite angry.

Of course, the key to making all this work is imagination. Just going through the motions isn't enough. You just can't fit into a few months the whole lifetime of experiences that your character would have had. With the disabled character, there was a lifetime of frustration and of dealing with people's reactions to the disability—experiences I just didn't have. So, to fill this gap, I had to use imagination. Even though my character was an adult, I spent a lot of time thinking through, imagining, how common childhood experiences would be different because of the disability; how that would have an emotional effect on the adult me. Because of course, people are shaped by their experiences. And this hard work paid off—I won an award for the role. What a celebration we had after that! We were partying for days!

But of course, personal experiences can be very, very useful for some roles. I played a London gang member once. Now, I'm not British, as you know, but I did have some experiences in my younger days with, shall we say, some of the less friendly people in New York. Some of these experiences helped me to understand what it feels like to be living on the edges of society. It wasn't exactly the same, of course, and you will never have exactly the same life experiences as your character. But, imagination is a way to fill that gap, too.

So, those are my thoughts. Any questions?

Student: Yes, Mr. Blake. I was wondering… on your first film…

UNIT 5

Psychology: Emotions

Previewing the Academic Skills Focus
Exercise 2, Page 76

Professor: One emotion that psychologists have studied a lot is fear. When someone is frightened, their heart beats faster, and they become more conscious of things around them. They become more alert, and concentrate harder. Their senses—their hearing, sight, smell, and sense of touch—become more sensitive. In short, they become ready for "fight or flight."

Lecture: Culture in Emotions

Professor: Good morning all, hello again. We'll continue with our topic of emotions. Today, we'll focus specifically on how we express emotions. We'll also look at where our emotional expression, our ways of expressing emotion, came from.

First of all, how are emotions expressed and communicated? To understand that, let's do a little thought experiment. Think about a good friend of yours. How do you know when he or she is surprised or angry? Do you wait for them to tell you, or can you just see it pretty easily? Unless the person is trying to hide their emotions, you can probably see their emotions before you hear them say anything. There are basically three channels for emotional expression: body movements and postures, facial expressions, and gestures.

Let's look at body movements first. These can be quite important in communicating emotions. Frequent body movements suggest emotional arousal, especially if they include touching, scratching, or rubbing. The faster the movement, the greater the level of arousal.

Postures also fall into the same category—let's call this category *body language*. For example, when someone is frightened, they might straighten their back and tighten their muscles. This is, of course, consistent with the "fight or flight" response. We might think that facial expressions—smiles, frowns, etc.—are the most obvious way to communicate emotions. However, research has shown the opposite. Meeren and other researchers in 2005 found that people usually judge emotion more by body language than by facial expression.

Speaking of facial expressions, let's look at them in more detail now. Clearly, if one of your friends smiles, you know they're happy. But is this the same around the world? To psychologists, this question is important for the following reason: Many think that emotional expression developed to help early humans survive. For example, expressing happiness could help people enjoy being with each other. Thus, they would stay together and be more likely to help each other through problems. However, if this theory is true, then most humans around the world would understand the same emotional expressions, as we all developed from these early humans.

Paul Ekman tried to find out. He traveled to meet a group of people who lived in a very remote part of Papua New Guinea. In fact, it was so remote that the people had met almost no one from other cultures. This was *exactly* what he wanted. He showed them pictures of people from cultures they had not met and did not know about. And guess what? They recognized some of the emotions *just* from the facial expressions. Through this and other experiments, he found something very interesting—for around six basic emotions, people from any culture can usually recognize the facial expressions. These basic emotions are sadness, happiness, anger, fear, disgust, and surprise. There is evidence that contempt and pride are also in this category, though not as much evidence as for the others.

Having said all that, of course there are differences in how people express emotions. This is often due to learning. For example, cultures often have rules for *when* people can display emotions. Psychologists call these *display rules*. People from some cultures, for instance, are less likely to display negative emotions with strangers. This doesn't mean that they feel emotions less strongly—it just means that they've learned when and where they can show them. Often these are part of the rules of politeness in the culture. Of course, not everyone from a particular culture follows the display rules.

Most gestures are also learned emotional responses, not instinct. Although they may generally reflect basic emotions, they often come from conscious decisions. For example, the "thumbs up" sign in many countries shows happiness with or approval of a decision or some news, but it is not as instinctive as a smile.

UNIT 6

Sociology: The Effects of Prosperity

Lecture: It Is the Best of Times

Professor: Good morning, everyone. Do you feel fortunate? Well, I certainly do. I feel fortunate to be alive *now*, in these modern times. Earlier this morning I sat down in my air-conditioned office, turned on my computer and answered e-mails from friends in Hong Kong and Scotland. To help me plan for tomorrow's trip, I checked the Tokyo weather forecast using the Internet, then I looked at a university database to find information for a book I'm writing. That may not sound like anything special, but compare it with the world I was born into, not much more than half a century ago. In that world, there were none of the things I've just mentioned—no Internet, no affordable, frequent jet airliners, no cell phones.

And it's not just technology that has changed our lives so much. Our average disposable income buys more than twice as much as it did in the mid-1950s. With our income, we have twice as many cars per person today compared with then. We eat at restaurants two and half times as often—and do plenty more besides.

And there's a lot more good news than just that.

- The U.S. population has doubled since 1945, but we produce triple the amount of food.
- Our pay can buy more. In 1919, a half a gallon of milk cost the average U.S. worker around 40 minutes of work. Eighty years later, that figure was only seven minutes.
- Heavy drinking rates and drunken driving deaths are decreasing.
- New medical treatments are saving more of us from diseases such as cancer.
- And life is getting safer. Look at car accidents, for example. The number of deaths per mile we drive halved from 1980 to 2006. This is just one example.

And what about family life? I wonder whether any of us really wish to experience the way families lived a hundred years ago. With outside toilets? With less electricity generated each year than we now use in a day? When people often died at an early age from diseases such as tuberculosis and pneumonia? During the twentieth century, life expectancy rose from 47 to 76 years.

A few years ago, a British TV company asked for families to volunteer for a reality TV show. They would spend three months living the middle-class life of 1900—which was probably very easy compared to working class life at the time. Out of 450 families who applied, the TV company chose Joyce and Paul Bowler and their four children. They had to get up at five thirty each morning, prepare food, wear uncomfortable clothes, shampoo with a smelly mixture including eggs and lemon, and play family games by gaslight at night. After just a week of this, they almost gave up. But they kept going. Perhaps a reason for their difficulties was that they didn't have people around them living a similar life. However, the reality of the early 1900s did not feel as romantic as they'd expected.

So, perhaps some people say we have problems in the present. But the past is *not* a golden age that we should try to bring back. Yesterday was not the best of times. Today is the best of times. Golden ages do happen, as political scientist John Mueller said … but they happen only in our memories. John Templeton sees the present as the best of times. In his book, *Is Progress Speeding Up?*, he concludes that things are getting better faster than ever, making this "a wonderful time to be alive!" How true. Yet there is more to the story. At the beginning of this lecture, I said I felt fortunate. However, I might not feel fortunate all the time …

Focused Listening

Exercise 5, Page 99

One: Do you feel fortunate? Well, I certainly do.

Two: Our average disposable income buys more than twice as much as it did in the mid-1950s.

Three: They would spend three months living the middle-class life of 1900—which was probably very easy compared to working class life at the time.

Four: Perhaps a reason for their difficulties was that they didn't have people around them living a similar life.

Five: The past is *not* a golden age that we should try to bring back.

Six: I might not feel fortunate all the time.

Before You Speak

Exercise 3, Page 107

Professor: OK, now you've just read the short piece about Bhutan. On the surface it seems to show that money doesn't always buy happiness. What do you think?

Student 1: Yes, it looks as though it is good evidence. I can certainly see how a countryside lifestyle is less stressful than modern life in richer countries.

Student 2: I see what you mean, but I can't agree, I'm afraid. I looked at the *Business Week* website, and most of the top ten countries in the survey were rich countries in Northern Europe. It looks as though Bhutan's just an exception to the normal rule.

Student 3: Yes, that could be true. But I think there's a problem with these surveys. Really, they don't tell you anything. Look at the list of the top eight countries: Denmark, Switzerland, Austria, Iceland, The Bahamas, Finland and Sweden, and of course, Bhutan. You could just as easily say that cold winters are important for happiness. Clearly there's no connection there.

Student 2: Interesting point, but it's hard to see a direct connection between winters and happiness. The connection between wealth and happiness is easier to see.

Student 1: Wealth may be common to some of them, but I noticed another one that seems to be common to even more of those top 10 countries in the survey. Most of them seem

to take steps to make sure there isn't a big gap between wealthy people and poor people. This includes Bhutan as well as the European countries. I read that equality is one of the features of the Gross National Happiness idea.

Professor: That's a very good point, but think also about the methodology of the study. Did anyone look into that? I think you'll find …

Focused Speaking

Exercise 1, Page 108

Professor: OK, now you've just read the short piece about Bhutan. On the surface it seems to show that money doesn't always buy happiness. What do you think?

Student 1: Yes, it looks as though it is good evidence. I can certainly see how a countryside lifestyle is less stressful than modern life in richer countries.

Student 2: I see what you mean, but I can't agree, I'm afraid. I looked at the *Business Week* website, and most of the top ten countries in the survey were rich countries in Northern Europe. It looks as though Bhutan's just an exception to the normal rule.

Student 3: Yes, that could be true. But I think there's a problem with these surveys. Really, they don't tell you anything. Look at the list of the top eight countries: Denmark, Switzerland, Austria, Iceland, The Bahamas, Finland and Sweden, and of course, Bhutan. You could just as easily say that cold winters are important for happiness. Clearly there's no connection there.

Student 2: Interesting point, but it's hard to see a direct connection between winters and happiness. The connection between wealth and happiness is easier to see.

Student 1: Wealth may be common to some of them, but I noticed another one that seems to be common to even more of those top 10 countries in the survey. Most of them seem to take steps to make sure there isn't a big gap between wealthy people and poor people. This includes Bhutan as well as the European countries. I read that equality is one of the features of the Gross National Happiness idea.

Professor: That's a very good point, but think also about the methodology of the study. Did anyone look into that? I think you'll find …

UNIT 7

Literature: Chinua Achebe

Lecture: Background on Chinua Achebe

Professor: Good morning, all. As you know, your next reading is *Marriage Is a Private Affair* by Chinua Achebe.

After that, you'll go on to read *Things Fall Apart*, one of his most famous novels. Some say it is the most popular African novel, and Achebe has been called "The father of modern African literature." *Things Fall Apart* was actually one of the first African novels to be published in the west.

To prepare for these readings, let's have a little look at some of the background. That will help you understand the story.

Achebe is one of the Igbo people from southeast Nigeria. His writing shows some of the big changes that his people have experienced over the last hundred years or so. These changes have resulted in some fascinating connections, connections between the old traditions and new beliefs. But to understand this, some history will help.

Originally, there was a strong and complex religion in Igboland. Then, the Europeans—first, the Portuguese, then the British—brought Christianity. Missionaries converted many locals to the new religion. In some areas, this happened only quite recently, just over a hundred years ago. However, many people kept some of the old traditions, and the result was a very complex mix of cultures: different villages—sometimes even different families in the same village—followed different combinations of the old and new beliefs. Often the cultures clashed—not always in a violent way, but confusion did happen. This is a strong theme in Achebe's writing, as you'll see.

One thing I want you to do is to look out for examples. Let's look at a couple to get you started. In *Marriage Is a Private Affair*, one of the characters, a young man named Nnaemeka, finds that his father has chosen a future wife for him. In other words, an arranged marriage. Arranged marriages are a part of the traditional culture. But, as many of you will know, they are not a central part of Christianity nowadays, at least in most countries.

And another example. You'll see that even the people in the village have a variety of reactions: they each have different opinions about dealing with Nnaemeka and the girl he wants to marry, Nene. Achebe himself has said that he does not want people to think of two cultures opposing each other, old against modern, or 'western' against African. Instead, he wants people to appreciate the amazing richness of thinking and behavior in his country. I think this way of thinking is a powerful idea, a great way to understand a society. Inside any country, you'll find many different cultures, even if people don't usually think of them as being different.

Now, for a little more background information, which will lead to another example. Lagos was the capital of Nigeria at the time the story was written, and one of the largest cities in Africa. Now, Nigeria has over 250 cultural groups, and people and families from all parts of Nigeria, from all of these cultural groups, came to live there. So it is a very diverse and complex city. Must be a fascinating place! Many people born in Lagos, like Nene, do not know much about the cultural traditions of the countryside. The problems caused by this lost knowledge is one of the themes of the story. Watch out for this when you read it.

It's interesting to think about whether the same issues may happen in other countries that are also changing very quickly—perhaps this country, perhaps your country if you're from overseas. Think about these things: How is society changing? What are the influences or causes of this change? How does this change the way generations communicate or interact with one another? By asking yourself these questions, you might relate better to the story. In this way, you might understand it better.

Anyway, I'm sure you'll enjoy the story.

Don't forget, though, to hand in your essays by the end of the week—the ones I assigned back at the beginning of the month. I don't want a repeat of last month's problems with lateness!

Focused Writing
Exercise 1, Page 122

Student: Nnaemeka was very upset about his father, Okeke's, sadness, and soon his trip came to an end. In the village, Okeke's neighbors came to visit the father, and all offered different opinions. One said, "It is the beginning of the end" when a son refuses to follow his father's wishes, and another quoted the Bible to justify this statement. Others suggested that Nnaemeka may have an illness of the mind, and a visit to a traditional healer would help, but Okeke didn't like that idea because it went against his Christian beliefs.

Six months later, Nnaemeka sent a picture of his recent wedding to Nene to his father. Okeke cut it in half and returned the part showing Nene. After that, father and son had little contact. In fact, Okeke tried hard to forget his son.

This went on for several years. Nnaemeka and Nene had two sons, who of course wanted to meet their grandfather. In the end, Nene couldn't hold herself back any longer. She wrote to Okeke, with a plan for the children to go to the village with Nnaemeka. Eventually, Okeke read the letter. Despite his stubbornness, not wanting to give up, he began to want to see the grandchildren.

UNIT 8

Earth Science: The Water Cycle

Previewing the Academic Skills Focus
Exercise 1, Page 130

Professor 1: It's terrible! The government really should do something to stop the Murray River from drying up.

Professor 2: Yes, the farmers are taking too much water. Whoever suggested they grow cotton in this country must have been crazy. The government needs to help them to change, to grow things that use less water.

Professor 1: Yep, we also have the same problem with rice.

Lecture: Human Intervention in the Water Cycle

Professor: Hello, everyone. Wonderful to see you all again. Hope you've been studying hard for tomorrow's test … and I hope you all do better this time! … Oh, yes, speaking of the test, don't forget to look carefully at chapter seven of your textbooks.

We're going to have a look today at the water cycle, and specifically, about how humans are changing it through their activities.

Several of the environmental problems we face at the moment come from our impacts on the water cycle. There are really four different types of impacts. One: changes to Earth's surface. Two: changes to Earth's climate. Three: air pollution. And four: withdrawals for human use.

First of all—changes to the surface of the Earth. Remember talking about how fast people were cutting down forests? Well, human effects on the water cycle may be even bigger. Now, I'll just quickly summarize what happens naturally, without much human activity—you're probably all familiar with this from high school. Diagram 8.1 in your notes shows all of this. In most natural systems, precipitation falls onto the ground. Some of the water soaks through to the groundwater reservoirs. This journey through the ground filters out dirt and microorganisms. Actually, it is because of this filtering that humans can drink the water— so, you can really see how important this filtering is. From the groundwater reservoirs, the water slowly moves through springs and enters streams and rivers, adding to their flow. The groundwater and springs help to keep rivers flowing, even in droughts. And the streams lead to rivers, lakes, and the sea, from where some of the water evaporates to form clouds. And so the cycle repeats.

Unfortunately, though, as humans cut down trees and overuse the land, the route of the water cycle changes. Water stops filtering through the ground. Instead, it runs straight into the streams or rivers. This sudden flow of water into waterways may not only cause floods, but also erode the land it flows over. This causes damage, and also brings more sediment and other pollution into the rivers.

Floods have always been common. However, in many parts of the world, they are now becoming more frequent. Also, the damage from them is getting worse. This is not because there is more rain, but because both tree cutting and farming have increased. Both of these human activities cause erosion and reduce filtering. More erosion means that more sediment comes down the river. The result is easy to see.

Events in Bangladesh give us a good example. That country is very flat. Most of the land is only a few meters above sea level. Clearly, then, flooding will have a terrible effect— something that has happened a lot in recent years and is likely to get worse. Extreme flooding is now common there. To find the reason, you have to travel hundreds and sometimes thousands of kilometers up the river to India and Nepal. There, people have cut down many trees from the lower parts of the Himalayan mountains. This has caused erosion, and the eroded material, the sediment, has washed down the river. Because of this, the Ganges River basin has risen between five and seven meters in recent years! A flood in 1998 covered 60 percent of the country and caused nearly a 1,000 deaths.

Also, when water just quickly runs off the ground rather then soaking through it or being taken up by trees, there is less water left to evaporate and cause local rainfall. Soon, springs will dry up as the supply to the groundwater reservoirs that feed them reduces. Dry and lifeless streams are common in areas with few trees. This has terrible results for both the ecosystems and the humans who depend on the flow.

Focused Listening

Exercise 1, Page 137

Professor: Now, I'll just quickly summarize what happens naturally, without much human activity—you're probably all familiar with this from high school. Diagram 8.1 in your notes shows all of this. In most natural systems, precipitation falls onto the ground. Some of the water soaks through to the groundwater reservoirs. This journey through the ground filters out dirt and microorganisms. Actually, it is because of this filtering that humans can drink the water—so, you can really see how important this filtering is. From the groundwater reservoirs, the water slowly moves through springs and enters streams and rivers, adding to their flow. The groundwater and springs help to keep rivers flowing, even in droughts. And the streams lead to rivers, lakes and the sea, from where some of the water evaporates to form clouds. And so the cycle repeats.

Exercise 2, Page 137

Professor: Unfortunately, though, as humans cut down trees and overuse the land, the route of the water cycle changes. Water stops filtering through the ground. Instead, it runs straight into the streams or rivers. This sudden flow of water into waterways may not only cause floods, but also erode the land it flows over. This causes damage, and also brings more sediment and other pollution into the rivers.

Exercise 3, Page 137

Professor: Unfortunately, though, as humans cut down trees and overuse the land, the route of the water cycle changes. Water stops filtering through the ground. Instead, it runs straight into the streams or rivers. This sudden flow of water into waterways may not only cause floods, but also erode the land it flows over. This causes damage, and also brings more sediment and other pollution into the rivers.

Exercise 4, Page 137

Professor: Floods have always been common. However, in many parts of the world, they are now becoming more frequent. Also, the damage from them is getting worse. This is not because there is more rain, but because both tree cutting and farming have increased. Both of these human activities cause erosion and reduce filtering. More erosion means that more sediment comes down the river. The result is easy to see.

Events in Bangladesh give us a good example. That country is very flat. Most of the land is only a few meters above sea level. Clearly, then, flooding will have a terrible effect—something that has happened a lot in recent years and is likely to get worse. Extreme flooding is now common there. To find the reason, you have to travel hundreds and sometimes thousands of kilometers up the river to India and Nepal. There, people have cut down many trees from the lower parts of the Himalayan mountains. This has caused erosion, and the eroded material, the sediment, has washed down the river. Because of this, the Ganges River basin has risen between five and seven meters in recent years! A flood in 1998 covered 60 percent of the country and caused nearly a 1,000 deaths.

Exercise 5, Page 138

Professor: Also, when water just quickly runs off the ground rather then soaking through it or being taken up by trees, there is less water left to evaporate and cause local rainfall. Soon, springs will dry up as the supply to the groundwater reservoirs that feed them reduces. Dry and lifeless streams are common in areas with few trees. This has terrible results for both the ecosystems and the humans who depend on the flow.

Exercise 6, Page 139

Excerpt One: Hope you've been studying hard for tomorrow's test … and I hope you all do better this time!

Excerpt Two: Oh, yes, speaking of the test, don't forget to look carefully at chapter seven of your textbooks.

Excerpt Three: We're going to have a look today at the water cycle, and specifically, about how humans are changing it through their activities. Several of the environmental problems we face at the moment come from our impacts on the water cycle. There are really four different types of impacts. One: changes to Earth's surface. Two: changes to Earth's climate. Three: air pollution. And four: withdrawals for human use.

Excerpt Four: Remember talking about how fast people were cutting down forests? Well, human effects on the water cycle may be even bigger.

Excerpt Five: Diagram 8.1 in your notes shows all of this.

Podcast: Disappearing Rivers Threaten Food Supply

The food supply of 2.4 billion people is under serious threat. Seven of the world's most important rivers, the Ganges, Indus, Brahmaputra, Yangtze, Mekong, Salween and the Yellow River, could disappear by 2035 due to global warming. These rivers begin in the glaciers of the Himalayas. They supply water to large populations in the two largest countries in the world, China and India, as well as Pakistan, Bangladesh, Afghanistan, Nepal, and Burma. In total, this covers a third of the world's population.

Due to global warming, the glaciers are melting. Already, floods in Bangladesh, India, and China are happening more often. As the glaciers melt, water flow will increase, causing even more flooding. Inevitably, this will make farming more difficult. Then, as the glaciers shrink, the supply of water to these important rivers will dry up, depriving millions of farmers of the water on which they grow rice and other crops. The consequences are real. So, why are we doing this?

Climate change is real … the effects will be dramatic … we need to take action … now!

Exercise 3, Page 141

1. The food supply of 2.4 billion people is under serious threat.

2. Due to global warming, the glaciers are melting.

3. So, why are we doing this?

4. Climate change is real…the effects will be dramatic…we need to take action…now!

Focused Speaking

Exercise 2, Page 141

Climate change is real … the effects will be dramatic … we need to take action … now!

CREDITS

Text credits: pp. 4-7, 11-13, *Biology: Science for Life with Physiology*, 2nd Edition, by C. Belk & V. Borden Maier, 2007. Pearson Benjamin Cummings, pp. 1-11. Used by permission.; **pp. 26-27, 31-32**, *Marketing: An Introduction*, 8th Edition, by G. Armstrong & P. Kotler, 2007. Pearson Prentice Hall, pp. 370-371, 376-77, 384, 452-453. p. 41, "Mass extinctions in the marine fossil record" in Science, 215, by David Raup and Jack Sepkoski, p. 1501-1503, 1982.; **pp. 43-44, 49-50**, *Astronomy Today*, 5th Edition, by E. Chaisson & S. McMillan, 2005. Pearson Prentice Hall, pp. 362-363.; **pp.59-60, 62-63**, *Acting: An Introduction to the Art and Craft of Playing*, by P. Kassel, 2007. Pearson Allyn & Bacon.; **pp. 79-80, 87**, *Psychology, AP Edition*, by P. Zimbardo, R. L. Johnson, A. L. Weber, & C. Gruber, 2007. Pearson Prentice Hall.; pp. 298-301.; **p. 92**, World Bank for 2007; CIA World Factbook, 2007; UN Development Program Report, 2007/2008; **pp. 95-95, 100-101**, "The Best of Times, the Worst of Times," in *The American Paradox: Spiritual Hunger in an Age of Plenty*, by David G. Myers, 2001. Yale University Press, pp. 1-12. Used by permission.; **p. 106**, "Bhutan" in *The World Factbook*, 2007. Central Intelligence Agency.; "The World Happiest Countries" in *Business Week*. Retrieved May 14, 2009, from http://images.businessweek.com/ss/06/10/happiest_countries/index_01.htm.; **pp. 115-116**, *Prentice Hall Literature: World Masterpieces*, Penguin Edition, 2007, pp. 1322-1339.; **pp. 118-119**, "Marriage Is a Private Affair" from *Girls at War and Other Stories* by Chinua Achebe, copyright © 1972, 1973 by Chinua Achebe. Used by permission of Doubleday, a division of Random House, Inc. and The Wylie Agency; **pp. 131-132, 136-138**, *Environmental Science: Toward a Sustainable Future*, 9th Edition, by R. Wright, 2005. Pearson Prentice Hall.

Photo credits: Cover: Art on File/Corbis; **p. 1** (TR) Shutterstock, (T) Shutterstock, (B) Shutterstock; **p. 4** Shutterstock; **p. 7** Shutterstock; **p. 12** Shutterstock, **p. 13** Shutterstock; **p. 15** (L) Shutterstock, (R) Shutterstock, (B) Shutterstock; **p. 16** (T) Shutterstock, (B) Shutterstock; **p. 17** (T) Shutterstock, (B) Shutterstock; **p. 21** (TR) Shutterstock, (M) David R. Frazier/PhotoEdit, (B) Reuters/Corbis; **p. 22** (L) Don Smetzer/PhotoEdit, (M) Shutterstock, (R) David R. Frazier/PhotoEdit; **p. 28** (L) Shutterstock, (B) Reuters/Corbis; **p. 32** David R. Frazier/PhotoEdit; **p. 39** (TR) Shutterstock, (background) Jim Zuckerman/Alamy, (T) B.A.E. Inc./Alamy, (M) Shutterstock, (B) Photodisc/Alamy; **p. 41** Jim Zuckerman/Alamy; **p. 43** Shutterstock; **p. 44** (T) Photodisc/Alamy, (M) Robert Harding Picture Library Ltd/Alamy; **p. 47** Paramount Pictures/Photofest; **p. 50** (T) B.A.E. Inc./Alamy, (B) Dr. Steve Gull & Dr. John Fielden/Photo Reseachers Inc; **p. 55** (TR) Shutterstock, (M) Robbie Jack/Corbis; **p. 56** (L) Universal Studios/Photofest, (R) NBC/Photofest; **p. 57** (L) Shutterstock, (R) New Line Cinema/Photofest; **p. 58** Shutterstock; **p. 59** Shutterstock; **p. 63** Sunset Boulevard/Corbis; **p. 67** (T) Polygram/The Kobal Collection, (B) DreamWorks/Photofest; **p. 69** Roger Bamber/Alamy; **p. 73** (TR) Shutterstock, (T) Imagebroker/Alamy, (M) Photo courtesy of Gosia Jaros-White, (B) Shutterstock; **p. 74** (L) Shutterstock, (R) Imagebroker/Alamy; **p. 75** Shutterstock; **p. 77** Shutterstock; **p. 79** Shutterstock; **p. 83** (L) Dorling Kindersley/Getty Images; **p. 87** Shutterstock; **p. 88** (T) Shutterstock, (B) Shutterstock; **p. 91** (TR) Shutterstock, (T) Shutterstock, (M) Shutterstock, (B) Digital Vision/Alamy; **p. 92** Digital Vision/Alamy; **p. 93** (L) Steve Allen Travel Photography/Alamy, (R) Shutterstock; **p. 96** PBS/Photofest; **p. 100** Shutterstock; **p. 103** Shutterstock; **p. 106** Shutterstock; **p. 108** Shutterstock; **p. 111** (TR) Shutterstock, (M) Ralph Orlowski/Reuters/Corbis; **p. 112** (L) Eddie Linssen/Alamy, (M) Lenscap/Alamy, (R) Barry Mason/Alamy; **p. 114** Ralph Orlowski/Reuters/Corbis; **p. 115** (T) Shutterstock, (B) Chad Henning/age fotostock; **p.116** Peter Jordan/Alamy; **p. 117** Fode Camara/Museum for African Art; **p. 127** (TR) Shutterstock, (background) Shutterstock, (T) Jack Sullivan/Alamy, (M) NOAA/Corbis, (B) Shutterstock; **p. 128** (TL) Shutterstock, (TR) Jack Sullivan/Alamy, (BL) Gideon Mendel/Corbis, (BR) NOAA/Corbis; **p. 130** Tony Hertz/Alamy; **p. 131** (L) Gerd Ludwig/Corbis, (R) ITPhoto/Alamy; **p. 132** (B) NASA/Alamy; **p. 134** Ern Mainka/Alamy; **p. 140** Shutterstock.

Illustrations: Dusan Petricic, **p. 2**; Gary Torrisi, **pp. 10, 62, 118, 136**

AUDIO CD TRACKING GUIDE